LIVES&
LEGACIES

Frida Kahlo

JACK RUMMEL

Frida Kahlo

A Spiritual Biography

A *Crossroad Book*
The Crossroad Publishing Company
New York

The Crossroad Publishing Company
370 Lexington Avenue, New York, NY 10017

First published in 2000 by The Crossroad Publishing Company

LIBRARY OF CONGRESS CATALOGING-IN-PUBLICATION DATA
Rummel, Jack
Frida Kahlo : a spiritual biography / Jack Rummel.
p. cm. – (Lives & Legacies)
Includes bibliographical references and index.
ISBN 0-8245-2353-9
1. Frida Kahlo. 2. Painters—Mexico—
Biography. I. Title.
ND259.K33 R86 2000
759.297—dc21
[B]   00-008212

Printed in the United States of America
Set in Janson
Designed and produced by SCRIBES Editorial
Cover design by Kaeser and Wilson Design Ltd.

Grateful acknowledgement is made to the following sources
for permission to reprint illustrations and photos:

AP/Wide World Photos
Corbis
Harry Ransom Humanities Research Center, University of
    Texas at Austin
Museum of Modern Art, New York
National Museum of American Art, Smithsonian Institution
Rockefeller Archive Center
Schalkwijk/Art Resource, NY
Throckmorton Fine Art, Inc.
University Art Gallery, New Mexico State University

Illustration and photo credits are given in the List of Illustrations following the
Bibliography.

1 2 3 4 5 6 7 8 9 10 03 02 01 00

CONTENTS

Frida Kahlo

Frida in the courtyard of the Blue House, ca. 1953.

1

Blue House

ON THE EVENING OF MAY 2, 1990, at Sotheby's auction house in New York City, a milestone was set in the history of Latin American art. For the first time a painting by an artist from that region broke the million-dollar sales mark. The painting, a small self-portrait that went for $1.43 million, was entitled *Diego and I.* It was completed in 1949 by the Mexican artist Frida Kahlo.[1]

It is unlikely that Kahlo would have been impressed by the auction at Sotheby's. For most of life she had been a committed Communist, and she probably would have written off this sale of her painting as a vulgar capitalist extravaganza. However, there is a good chance she would have been pleased with the symbolism of the event. It marked her work as belonging among the finest of her peers, a group composed almost exclusively of men—Picasso, Matisse, Dali, and Kandinsky, to name a few.

During her life, Frida Kahlo was only a marginally successful painter. She had just two solo art shows, one in New York in 1938, and another in Mexico City in 1953, a little more than a year before her death. Her works did not sell easily, and she was often broke and much to her chagrin had to rely on "loans" from her husband, the famed Mexican muralist Diego Rivera, to get by. When she did sell her paintings, she was lucky to get a few hundred dollars for one (in 1938 actor Edward G. Robinson bought four from her for two hundred dollars each). Her works actually sank in value for a period in the 1950s and early 1960s. Much more than as an artist, she was known as a celebrity, but only a minor one—the moon reflected in the dazzling burst of her famous and egomaniacal husband.

In spite of the scant attention she received in her life, Frida Kahlo was not destined to sink into obscurity. Rivera continued to champion her until his death in 1957. The house where she was born and in which she lived for much of her life was converted into a national museum in 1958.

Slowly word of her paintings and of her extraordinary life filtered down to a new generation, one that would be profoundly transformed by the feminist movement of the 1960s and 1970s. For this generation, and especially its women, Frida Kahlo would become a cult figure, a symbol of a talent ignored, a woman betrayed not only by patriarchal authority but by fate itself. The story of her horrendous physical suffering, her debilitating accident and subsequent torment at the hands of doctors, would convert her into something like a female Christ figure. That she captured the events of her life in a series of surreal and transfiguring paintings only added a richer glow to her mythical aura.

Unfortunately, the public at large rarely had a chance to see Kahlo's paintings. To see her works, you had to travel to the Frida Kahlo Museum in Mexico City. The museum never loaned out its collection and her other paintings only rarely popped up in galleries in Mexico, Europe, or the United States. This changed with a show organized by the Mexican government in 1977. At last, a retrospective was available that showed the evolution of her paintings, and the trajectory of her life, from the late 1920s until her death in 1954. This show was followed by another, in the United States in 1978–79 that traveled to six museums, and a show of her work in England in 1982. The 1990 Sotheby's sale merely put an exclamation mark on a frenzy of Fridamania that continued to grow in the United States and Europe during the 1980s.

The Sotheby's sale of 1990 confirmed an irony. It has been Kahlo's work, more than that of her husband's or many of the other recognized male artists of her lifetime, that has not only endured, but has triumphed. Forty-six years after her death, Frida Kahlo has become the most famous twentieth-century artist of Latin America and one of the most famous artists in the world.

Frida Kahlo also has come to occupy a passionate role in discussions and issues of constructions of identity among individuals and groups the world over. Her importance to artists in Mexico, especially—is indisputable and far-reaching. And according to Liza Bakewell, author of *Frida Kahlo: A Contemporary Feminist Reading*, "Her popularity worldwide is particularly noteworthy in regard to contemporary feminist issues concerned with the relationship of gender to race, class, and ethnicity."

At first glance, Frida Kahlo, Communist, atheist, bohemian vivant, would not seem the most likely candidate for a series of biographies whose individual works examine not only the lives but the spirituality of their subjects. She belittled traditional religious beliefs, embraced materialist Communist doctrine, and often seemed to revel in breaking taboos. Yet if spirituality is understood to be the coupling of a quest for self-understanding with an impatience for, and outspokenness against, injustice and political oppression, that is, an unending search for oneself and one's place in the world, then Frida Kahlo was a deeply spiritual person. Through her paintings she found the language that would eventually impel her to tell her story, unflinchingly charting her personal and spiritual quest and suffering.

Much of Frida's talent for detecting complacency and her sharp eye for uncovering hypocrisy came to her through her father, Wilhelm Kahlo, a German Jew whose failed attempts to fit into Mexican society, and whose strong German accent was never lost, equipped him with an outsider's eye for its defects. The elder Kahlo was born in Baden Baden in 1872 and at birth was already something of an outsider in Germany. He was Jewish in a nation that had never completely accepted Jews as full citizens. He was also a child of immigrants; his parents, Jakob and Henriette, had only recently moved to Germany from Arad, a town then a part of the Austro-Hungarian Empire (now part of Rumania) that held a sizeable Hungarian-speaking population as well as Rumanians, Gypsies, Slavs, and some Gentile Germans and German-speaking Jews.

Undoubtably Jakob and Henriette Kahlo were drawn to Germany by its prospering economy and to Baden Baden in particular because of the wealthy clientele who came to its spas. In Baden Baden, Jakob Kahlo set up a jewelry store and also supplied photographic supplies as a side business. Wilhelm must have been a relatively talented student; his grades were good enough to win him admission to the University of Nuremberg in 1889 or 1890. That Jakob had enough money to send his son to a university indicates that he had prospered in Germany. At this point in a placid scenario there is no reason to believe that Wilhelm would not receive a degree, enter a profession or take over the family business, and settle into German life a happy and prosperous member of its bourgeoisie.

Yet this sketchy factual picture, which is about all the taciturn Wilhelm Kahlo ever gave to his family in Mexico, is misleading, for in 1891 he suddenly quit the university and took a steamer bound for the Mexican port of Veracruz. Jakob purchased the ticket for his son, but gave him little else with which to start a new life in a foreign country. Essentially, Wilhelm Kahlo, son of a prosperous German businessman, arrived broke at the port of Veracruz. Apparently though, he had at least one thing going for him on entry to Mexico. Either he had persuaded two friends, the Diener brothers, to come with him, or he had known they were leaving and tagged along with them. They would be his lifeline during the first crucial years in this strange, new country.

According to Wilhelm this sudden exodus from Germany was the result of a fall he had taken while at the university, which had left him with recurring bouts of epilepsy and made further study difficult. He also mentioned that his mother had recently died and his father had quickly remarried. Apparently the new wife and the stepson did not get along, and at this point the hot-headed Wilhelm decided to toss in his education and flee to the wilds of Mexico.

This story leaves out more than it tells: the likelihood that father and son had a troubled relationship far earlier than the father's remarriage, the possibility of a strained marriage between Jakob and Henriette, and the probability that Wilhelm Kahlo had been an epileptic most of his life. Perhaps some combination of shame and anger, precipitated by his mother's death, finally caused him to impulsively leave his home and strike out on his own. In 1891, there was scarcely a more far-removed place than Mexico, exotic and flush with possibility in the European imagination, for a young German to head to in search of a new life. On arrival Wilhelm became Guillermo. He never returned to Germany.

Mexico had not always seemed a promising destination for immigrants. An independence movement begun in 1810 by the priest Miguel Hidalgo, along with many wealthy Mexicans of Spanish descent, called creoles, decided to side with Spanish royal authorities rather than risk losing their properties to a revolution that had become increasing radical. Independence only came in 1822 when the militia in Mexico revolted against a new, liberal government in Spain.

From the beginning, the new Mexican government was ultraconservative and unstable. Political participation in Mexico for the next forty years was a time during which fifty-six different governments passed through a revolving door that led them swiftly in and out of power. Bloodshed, tyranny, corruption, and gross social inequality were Mexico's distinguishing features during these times. The one constant was the continuing privilege of the creole elite and the Catholic Church, both of whom lived off the labor, under conditions not far removed from slavery, of their Indian and mestizo workers.

Mexico's most famous and progressive leader during this period was Benito Juárez. A Zapotec Indian from the state of Oaxaca, Juárez fought through several civil wars before bringing a liberal, constitutional government to power in Mexico City in 1867. Inspired by the United States Constitution, Juárez and his fellow liberals wrote Constitutional articles guaranteeing separation of Church and State, freedom of religion, and free education for all regardless of social class.

But Juárez would only govern for five year before dying of cancer in 1872. He was eventually succeeded in 1876 by his most successful general, Porfirio Díaz, who during a dictatorship lasting thirty-four years finally brought the stability and—to a few—the prosperity the Mexican people had been seeking since Independence.

However, in his headlong pursuit of economic development, Díaz largely abandoned Juárez's liberal, reform initiatives. The

Church stealthily regained its lands and power, while foreign companies were granted huge government contracts to modernize the county's infrastructure, most notably its railways, which were built by American and British companies from the 1870s. Saddest of all, Díaz let languish Juárez's ambitious program of education reform. By 1895, four years after Guillermo Kahlo immigrated to Mexico, government statistics revealed that only 18 percent of Mexico's population was literate.[2]

In coming to Mexico, Guillermo Kahlo was riding a tide that rewarded economic gain to uppercrust Mexicans and educated foreigners. It was not unusual to see foreign faces in supervisory and management positions at many businesses. As long as the foreigners were white, things foreign were lauded as being superior to native Mexican workers and institutions. One Mexican legislator in 1890 remarked that he was happy "to see that foreigners owned the banks, the credit institutions, the electric light companies, the telegraph, the railways and everything that signifies culture and progress in Mexico."[3]

In spite of his huge relative advantage over the vast majority of the Mexican population, Guillermo Kahlo's first few years in Mexico were spent in a sort of restless semi-poverty. He first worked as a cashier at a German-owned glassware store, then as a salesman at a book shop. Three years after his arrival, he began to work with his fellow countrymen, the Diener brothers at La Perla, a jewelry store they established in Mexico City soon after their arrival, and apparently felt secure enough about his future that he married a Mexican woman and started a family. On the birth of her second daughter in 1898, Kahlo's first wife died. At roughly the same time, Kahlo fell in love with a fellow employee at La Perla, a young woman named Matilde Calderón.

Calderón was a *mestiza*, a woman of mixed European and Indian ancestry. Her mother was the daughter of a Spanish general who had remained in Mexico after Spanish imperial rule in Mexico collapsed in 1822, and her father was an Indian from the state of Morelos. Matilde was born in Oaxaca, her mother's hometown, but like so many other ambitious but financially insecure Mexicans, the Calderóns were drawn by the promise of opportunity to Mexico City, settling there in the late 1870s.

Matilde Calderón's father, Antonio, brought with him to Mexico City his photography business, at which he was apparently talented, if not as an artist at least as an artisan and a businessman. By the time Guillermo Kahlo and Matilde Calderón wed, Antonio Calderón and his family seem to have risen into a comfortable if not shaky position amid the city's middle class. Antonio immediately brought his son-in-law into the trade and gradually Guillermo Kahlo took over the business. He proved to be at least as industrious and probably more talented than his father-in-law, although he had an aversion to photographing members of the burgeoning middle class, remarking wryly that he "did not want to photograph people because he did not wish to improve on what God had made ugly."[4] Instead, Guillermo Kahlo preferred taking pictures of buildings, offices, landscapes, and factories.

Guillermo, and by extension the Kahlo family, were briefly catapulted into the upper middle class when Guillermo was chosen in 1904 to be the official government photographer of Mexico's colonial and pre-Columbian architecture. Kahlo was selected by none other than José Ives Limantour, the cunning and able finance minister to Mexican dictator Porfirio Díaz, and the leading intellectual voice for Díaz's policy of seeking foreign investment and immigration at the expense of the majority of the Mexican people. Guillermo Kahlo was to become the "first official photographer of Mexico's cultural patrimony."

The project, which culminated in a book and exhibition in 1910, the one-hundredth anniversary of the declaration of Mexican Independence, was a great coup. With this windfall, Kahlo was able to buy a piece of land several blocks from the plaza of Coyoacán, which for most of its existence had been a separate town beyond the outskirts of Mexico City, but which by the early 1900s was being engulfed in the city's growth. On this lot, in a pleasant, sleepy suburb, he built a rambling rock and adobe house in the Mexican colonial style—single-story, and like most Mexican houses, facing inward, a place of familial refuge, with rooms whose doors open onto a sunny inner courtyard. The outside walls were painted a deep blue, a feature that gave the house its name, La Casa Azul, the Blue House.

Magdalena Carmen Frieda Kahlo y Calderón was born in the Blue House on July 6, 1907. She was the third Kahlo daughter and was largely cared for by her two older sisters, and occasionally by her half-sisters from Guillermo Kahlo's first marriage who had been sent to live in a convent when Kahlo had married Matilde. It is likely that the decision to send the older daughters off to convent was made by Matilde Kahlo. By most accounts, she seems early on to have been, if not bitter, then at least disappointed by life. She married at twenty-four—late for a woman at that time in Mexico—and later confided to Frida that the true love of her life had been another German youth she had known who had committed suicide before she had met Guillermo Kahlo. Guillermo had been very much a second choice; an intelligent, hard-working man, respected but apparently never loved by his wife.

Daily life at the Blue House seems to have been regulated and gloomy. Frida's half-sisters remembered a place dominated by Matilde, a "small-minded, vain, and selfish woman." Other members of the Kahlo's extended family recall an empty house in which Guillermo and Matilde "were always disappearing behind heavy wooden doors."[5] Later in her life, Frida recalled that

Guillermo Kahlo, ca. 1893.

Frida (standing), her mother (sitting center), flanked by sisters Adriana, (left), Matilde (right), Cristina (sitting on ground left), and other extended family members, 1928.

my mother was a friend of gossips, the children, and the old women who used to come by the house to pray their rosaries. . . . I remember that my mother was never in need of anything; she always had five silver pesos stashed away in her bureau drawer. . . . She was a short woman with beautiful eyes, a very fine mouth, and dark skin—she was like a Oaxacan bellflower. . . . Mama was very congenial, active, intelligent, but didn't know how to read or write, only count money.[6]

In spite of what Frida said about her mother being "congenial" and "active," by the time Frida was born, Matilde seems to have begun a subtle emotional withdrawal from her family. Frida's younger sister Cristina was conceived only a few months after Frida's birth and the pregnancy proved so physically difficult for Matilde that she handed Frida over to an Indian wet nurse for breastfeeding. Later, Matilde began to be plagued by attacks that were similar to Guillermo's epileptic fits, which caused her to frequently take to her bed. For much of their youth, Frida and her younger sister Cristina were raised by their older sisters Matilde and Adriana as their mother became increasingly devout and remote. "My mother," Frida said, "was a great friend to me, but the religious thing never brought us close to each other; she would reach the point of hysteria for her religion. We had to pray before meals, and while the rest were concentrating, Cristi and I would look at each other trying not to laugh."[7]

Guillermo Kahlo was scarcely less stoic than his wife, but he seems to have developed a special affection for his third daughter. He called her "Frida lieber" and believed her "the most intelligent of my daughters. She is the most like me."[8] Early on, perhaps by nine or ten, Frida began helping her father on some of his commercial photography outings. By then, the family could fairly well predict the timing of Guillermo's epileptic seizures (about every five to six weeks), and Frida would accompany him if she thought he was near having an attack.

"He would suddenly fall down while walking with his camera slung over his shoulder and holding my hand," Frida later remembered. "I learned how to help him during his attacks in the middle of the street. On one hand I was careful to have him breathe ether or alcohol right away and on the other I kept close watch so that nobody would steal his photographic equipment."[9]

Guillermo Kahlo maintained a rigid, old-world work schedule, leaving early for the long tram ride into central Mexico City where his studio was located, and returning late, always at the same hour, around eight in the evening. His studio—with its set-pieces of French furniture, oriental rugs, and various bucolic landscape backdrops for portraits; large Hasselbach and Graflex cameras; books in German of Schiller, Goethe, and German philosophers— was an enclosed Middle European bubble lovingly constructed amid the dusty bustle of the city. Back home in the evening, he retreated to the parlor, closed its doors, and played Beethoven, Mozart, or Strauss, for one hour precisely. Then he went to the dining room and ate alone in silence while his wife waited on him.

It was the life of a lonely man with few friends. According to Frida, Guillermo Kahlo wanted to become part of Mexican society, but his obvious foreignness, prickly sense of pride, and the difficulty of making connections in a large city prevented him from ever feeling that Mexico was more than a waystation through life.

Guillermo did occasionally set aside his inflexible schedule to be with Frida. He was a weekend painter and liked to take her to parks while he worked on a watercolor. Noticing that she liked to collect insects, stones, and plants on these outings, Guillermo stimulated Frida's intellectual adventureness and encouraged her to study nature and lent her books on biology and geology from his library. He also owned a microscope, which back at the Blue House Frida would use along with the books he lent her to identify specimens she had found. Later he taught her the intricacies of the camera and techniques to use when developing film.

These early influences left an impression on her life and work. When she was in high school, she developed an intense interest in biology and human physiology and planned to become a doctor. Later, when she had switched her career to painting, her self-portraits often displayed the formal, even deliberately stilted, sensibility of her father's photography.

The attention and encouragement from her father were Frida's happiest childhood moments, but there were several other, bleaker episodes that show a household in disarray and a child in distress. When Frida was seven her oldest sister Matilde, then fifteen, ran away from home with her boyfriend, an act in which Frida claimed she was an accomplice:

> I helped my sister Matilde escape to Veracruz with her boyfriend. I opened the balcony door for her and then shut it as if nothing had happened. Because Matita was my mother's favorite, her flight made Mamá hysterical. What made Matita want to leave? My mother was hysterical because she didn't know. . . .
>
> When Mati went away, my father didn't say a word. . . . We spent four years without seeing Matita, and while we were in a streetcar one day, my father said, "We'll never find her!" I consoled him, and my hopes were really sincere. I was twelve years old when a friend from the Preparatory School told me: "On the street where the doctors live there's a woman who looks exactly like you and her name is Matilde Kahlo." At the back of the patio, in the fourth room of a wide hallway, I found her. She was living there with Paco Hernán-

dez, whom she had married. . . . The first thing I did was tell my father I'd found her. I visited her several times and tried to convince my mother to see her, but she refused.[10]

Besides revealing the older Matilde's stubbornness, and the fractures this caused in her family, this remembrance is curious for another reason. Frida had become aware of her sister's whereabouts because she knew this area, "the street where the doctors live." By twelve, she was already an old hand with physical pain, ailments, afflictions, and doctors.

The young Frida's first medical crisis came in 1913 when she was six. That year, according to a statement she gave later to another doctor, she stubbed her right foot against a tree stump. Afterward, she fell ill and was confined to her room for nine months. "It all started with a terrible pain in my right leg, from the thigh downward. They'd soak my little leg in a small tub of walnut water and hot cloths, and the poor little leg stayed very thin. At seven I used small boots [to align my legs properly]."[11]

At first the doctors weren't sure what was wrong with her. One set of doctors diagnosed the illness as "white tumors"; another set believed it was polio. The second set was right. Frida had contracted a serious viral disease, but not from hitting her foot against a tree. The muscles of her leg atrophied, the foot turned inward slightly, and the affected leg became a touch shorter than the other. In 1913, there was little doctors could do for polio. Besides the hot walnut oil baths, the young patient was ordered to take large doses of calcium and lie in the sun as much as possible.

She was lucky the illness affected her so little. At that time, and until a vaccine for polio was developed in the 1950s, polio outbreaks killed thousands of children and seriously disabled thousands more each year. By comparison, Frida was fortunate.

The illness frightened her, but within the straitened emotional atmosphere of the Blue House she wasn't able to express her fears. Instead she learned the stoicism of her parents and, as she recalled later in her diary, comforted herself with the creation of an imaginary friend:

> I must have been 6 years old when I experienced intensely an imaginary friendship with a little girl more or less the same age as me. On the glass window of what at that time was my room, . . . I breathed vapor onto one of the first panes. I let out a breath and with a finger drew a "door." . . .
>
> Full of great joy and urgency, I went out in my imagination, through this "door." I crossed the whole plain that I saw in front of me until I arrived at a dairy called "Pinzón." I entered the "O" of Pinzón and I went down in great haste into the *interior of the earth* where my imaginary friend was always waiting for me. . . . She was gay—she laughed a lot. Without sounds. She was agile and she danced as if she weighed nothing at all. I followed her in all her movements and while she danced I told her my secret problems. . . . When I returned . . . I ran with my secret and my joy to the farthest corner of the patio of my house, and always in the same place under a cedar tree, I cried out and laughed at being alone with my great happiness.[12]

When the worst of her illness was over, Frida began to reconstruct herself physically and emotionally. Her doctors urged her to take up physical exercise to rehabilitate her leg. Encouraged by her father, she took up all kinds of sports. She tried bicycling, soccer, swimming, even boxing and wrestling—all unusual for a girl from proper Mexican society.

Some of the neighborhood children would torment her,

yelling "pata de palo" (peg leg) at her as she rode by on her bike. "At first I assumed that the children's taunts wouldn't affect me," she said later, "but later they really did, and each time worse."[13]

Nonetheless, wearing a right shoe with a slightly raised heel and multiple socks to make her leg seem thicker, she soldiered on, her sense of distinctness and vulnerability heightened, and her determination to prove herself intensified. These sensibilities would stay with her throughout her life.

Frida at eighteen, 1926.

2

Carnival of Skulls

Here was the psychological mold of the new Mexican, which gave
his mind its fundamental shape, and made him reject all authority
as openly as he dared.

—Justo Sierra

IN SEPTEMBER 1910, when Frida was three years old, Porfirio
Díaz, the long-reigning dictator of Mexico, staged a month-long
extravaganza in Mexico City to celebrate the hundredth anniversary of Mexican Independence—and also, as some of his critics
noted—his own eightieth birthday. Glittering new hotels were
built along Paseo de la Reforma, the tree-shaded boulevard that
was the pride of the city's elite, and the government offered
thousands of foreign visitors and press correspondents junkets to
Mexico City to view the occasion. Dozens of balls were thrown
during the month by Mexico City's established families. Even
the city's innumerable poor were included, although in an odd,
backhanded way: thousands of pairs of new pants were distrib-
uted to poor men who were told to wear them during the celebrations instead of their traditional white cotton pantaloons as a
way of showing foreigners that "progress" had trickled down
even to the common folk. So lavish were the festivities, and so
skewed the government's priorities, that more money was paid
for the centennial celebrations than for the 1910 national education budget.

The centennial celebrations were supposed to have been the apogee of the Porfiriato, as the reign of Porfirio Díaz was called, a popular affirmation of Díaz's thirty-year-plus program of "Order and Progress." Yet more than a few observers detected the hollowness at the centennial's core. As noted by Frederick Starr, president of the University of Chicago and one of the government's invited guests, "Thousands thronged to watch the passing show, yet there was no outburst of delight. Porfirio Díaz, brilliant with royal decorations, and distinguished guests swept by without applause."[1]

There were deep and widespread reasons for this lack of popular enthusiasm, which echoed through Frida's childhood, youth, and beyond. One of the most resented and corrosive elements of Mexico's economic transformation under Porfirio Díaz was the ideology of social Darwinism that had been officially embraced by the government. The pseudoscientific theories of this bleak social contract had been developed in Europe by the French sociologist Auguste Comte and applied in Mexico by a group of Díaz's top advisors called the *científicos*. The *científicos*, led by Díaz's finance minister, José Ives Limantour, believed that Darwin's discoveries about natural selection could be fitted to an analysis of societies, and that, as in the natural world studied by Darwin, a "survival of the fittest" could also be attained in human affairs. Limantour stated his clique's positivistic creed most baldly when he asserted that, "the weak, the unprepared, those who lack the necessary tools to triumph in the evolutionary process, must perish and leave the field to the strongest."[2]

Científico policies made an already sharp social divide even starker. Most federal expenditures to improve standards of living—money spent for road paving, water treatment, electrical production—went to wealthy neighborhoods in the large cities, especially Mexico City. The poor in Mexico City, the majority of whom lived in desperate slums on the dried-up bottom of what had been Lake Texcoco on the city's east side, got nothing. Here immigrants fresh from the Mexican countryside crowded into *vecinidades*, one- or two-story tenements where a dozen or more people might share a single unfurnished room. Many others lived on the streets.

There was neither any sewage system in these barrios, nor running water, nor clean water of any kind. The streets themselves were the sewers, and unclean water had to be hauled from communal wells located nearer to the city center. Work was hard to find and paid less than a living wage when it could be scrounged up. Many men worked as *cargadores*, human draught animals who hauled carts of goods around the city.

During the summer rainy season, the dry lakebed filled with water, which meant that much of the east side flooded and remained that way for months. Streets became "black-water lakes that interrupt traffic, stall commerce, and let off horrible smelling and deadly gases that force the people to cover their noses. . . . to quell the nausea."[3]

By 1910, when Frida was three years old, "this cesspool of a city," was thought even by its inhabitants to be "the most unhealthy city in the world."[4] More than eight thousand children died in the city every year and mortality rates were twice as high as Rio de Janiero and Buenos Aires, and higher even than Cairo and Madras, India. The great majority of these deaths occurred on the east side and in other poor barrios.

The greatest visual chronicler of this age was a man named José Guadalupe Posada, who worked for the publisher Antonio Vanegas Arroyo in Mexico City from 1888 until 1913, the year of his death. Posada illustrated thousands of broadsheets that were issued from the Vanegas Arroyo printing house. These were typically a single sheet of paper printed on both sides that dealt with topics—murders, suicides, bandits and other folk heroes, natural disasters—popular with the poor, mass audience that Vanegas Arroyo targeted.

Posada's illustrations were usually accompanied by text—sometimes straight stories about actual events; other times *corridos*, the lyrics of folk ballads; and often fictional short stories reputing to tell details about the lives of typical Mexico City residents. Posada often reserved the harshest treatment not for the very wealthy and who benefitted the most from Díaz's economic policies, but the city's new middle class, just one shaky rung up from the slum dwellers. His sensibilities—especially his use of the *calavera*, or skeleton figure—to mock social pretensions, even death itself, would later exert great influence on Frida Kahlo.

In politics, José Limantour's call to leave "the field to the strongest" meant a disregard for democracy and human rights. "Rights! Society now rejects them," trumpeted a *científico* paper ironically named *La Libertad*. "What it wants is bread, . . . a little less of rights in exchange for a little more in security, order, and peace. We have already enacted innumerable rights, which produce only distress and malaise in society. Now let us try a little tyranny, but honorable tyranny, and see what results it brings."[5]

The "results" came with shocking speed on the heels of Díaz's centennial celebrations. Within a month of the end of the this orgy of self-congratulation, a little-known politician named Francisco Madero escaped from house arrest and fled to San Antonio, Texas, where in November 1910, he issued a *grito*, or decree (literally "shout"), declaring himself the new president of a provisional revolutionary government.

Madero, who was the son of wealthy *hacendados* from northern Mexico, had been the only politician brave or deluded enough to challenge Díaz on his eighth re-election bid in the summer of 1910. His bid to overthrow the old dictator came at

The *Calaveras* of José Guadalupe Posada

The son of a baker from the central Mexican city of Aguascalientes, Posada's natural artistic talent led to his apprenticeship at sixteen to an engraver in the city of his birth. His satirical cartoons, published as illustrations in broadsheets and local newspapers, soon got him into trouble. Within a few years he had to move to another town to escape a jail sentence when he criticized a local politician.

By 1888 Posada had made his way to Mexico City where he sat up shop in the center of the metropolis at 220 Calle de la Moneda, just a few blocks from the Zócalo. Working with the publisher Vanegas Arroyo, Posada illustrated thousands of broadsheets and newspapers that were aimed primarily at a working-class audience.

Some of Posada's most intriguing and influential prints are *calaveras*, or skeletons. Skeleton figures had been used in European art to signify death since the Middle Ages. However, Posada put a distinctly Mexican slant on his *calaveras*. Wearing suits and ties, top hats, or decked out in sombreros and other Mexican garb, they express a simultaneous defiance and embrace of death that is found only in Mexico. They drink, dance, carouse, ride the newly installed electric trolleys. Attached to most etchings is a narrative that tells a story pertinent to Posada's working-class readership.

In portraying the skeleton figure in this way Posada was drawing on deep Mexican roots, ancient Aztec and other indigenous traditions in which death is mocked or venerated, but is always recognized as an integral part of life. The *calavera* etchings also offered Posada a way to make indirect political comments about events of the day. If the persons represented in a commentary about a corrupt public works deal or deplorable social conditions were skeletons and not actual people, it would be more difficult to prosecute the artist on charges of undermining the authority of the government.

Posada drew thousands of prints during his fifteen years in Mexico City, yet he died virtually unheralded. Diego Rivera claimed to have studied with him, although this is almost certainly not true. However, another great Mexican muralist and painter, José Clemente Orozco, did know of Posada during his heyday. Orozco passed by Posada's shop on his way to and from elementary school and often stopped to look at the broadsheets that had been hung in the window. "This was the first jolt that awakened my imagination, and led me to scribble on paper my first outlines," Orozco said. "[Posada was] the first revelation to me of the existence of the art of painting."

exactly the right time for opponents of the old regime. Disgust with *científico* rule ignited widespread support for Madero, especially in the north of the country.

For the next nine years, the years of Frida's childhood, revolution and warfare engulfed Mexico. Idealism and hope for social change were frequently met with treachery and betrayal. Francisco Madero, the idealist, vegetarian teetotaler who had assumed the presidency after the fall of Díaz, lasted slightly more than a year and a half before he was assassinated on orders of his own army chief of staff. This general held power for another year and he too was ousted. Between 1915 and 1919, the country was often divided between warlords, two of the strongest being the former outlaw Francisco "Pancho" Villa, and the peasant leader Emiliano Zapata.

The countryside was especially devastated by the movements of competing armies, but Mexico City even though it had been occupied several times by different armies, survived more or less intact. However, the revolution impoverished the Kahlo household. With the collapse of the Díaz government, Guillermo Kahlo's government contracts evaporated. He had to scramble for work, getting back into the distasteful business of taking portraits of "those whom God had made ugly." Matilde Kahlo was forced to let go of her servants and carefully apportion the household's money. Nonetheless, compared to the dire poverty that persisted in many parts of the city, the Kahlo's lived well, if insecurely, in a state of genteel scruffiness.

Frida remembered the years of the civil war with excitement, if not always with strict accuracy:

During the Tragic Decade [the Revolution] my mother would open the balcony windows . . . and welcome the Zapatistas.

She'd attend to their wounds and give the hungry thick corn tortillas, the only food she could find in Coyoacán those days. . . . The clear and precise emotion I remember about the Mexican Revolution made me join the Young Communists at the age of thirteen, but in 1914 the bullets began to hiss. I can still hear their extraordinary sound.[6]

Undoubtably, Frida saw Zapatistas in the streets of her neighborhood. They occupied the capital in November 1914 and, with Villa's forces, stayed there until March the following year. But her claim to have joined the Young Communist League in 1920 at age thirteen is almost certainly untrue. She was still well within the clutches of the Church and her family at that time.

Still, the five months between November 1914 and March 1915, and the several following it, were times of confusion and anarchy in the capital. Villa's forces went on a manhunt to track down and execute anyone who opposed or offended them. The Zapatistas, too, often took the law into their own hands and were especially rough on suspected criminals. In one incident, three men were hanged outside a police station. On the body of the first man, the Zapatistas pinned a note: "This man was killed for being a thief." A note of the second man read: "This man was killed for printing counterfeit money." The note on the third man said simply: "This man killed by mistake."[7] This sort of grim black humor was brought to a high art during the Revolution.

In all, more than a million people died during this ten-year maelstrom of revolution and counterrevolution. By 1920, two years before Frida would enter the Escuela Preparatoria, the disorder and confusion in the capital and the countryside had ended. A more stable leadership under former generals Alvaro Obregón and Plutarco Calles had emerged. Gone were Zapata, who had been murdered in an ambush in 1919, and Villa, who had been bought off with the peace offering of a large ranch in the state of Chihuahua.

The new leaders, Obregón and Calles, emphasized that they were fashioning a new nation out of the ruins of the old. The new government used all the tools of propaganda at its disposal to bill itself as "revolutionary," and emphasized that it stood for land reform, industrial development to modernize Mexico, fair wages and decent working conditions for workers. Yet, these claims and promises were by and large worthless. The government did promote industrialization and supported a state-controlled labor union, but few properties owned by large *hacendados* were returned to peasant farmers. More often properties were simply confiscated and given intact to Obregón and Calles's friends and cronies, who became the new Mexican aristocracy. Most of the other promises were delivered only in small bits and pieces to placate the organizers of occasional protest.

However, for a while in the early 1920s, Alvaro Obregón managed to enlist a few prominent intellectuals as ministers in his government. Among artists and intellectuals there was still a stirring of hope for revolutionary change, and there was a feeling on the part of many Mexican intellectuals that the Russian and Mexican revolutions were the first acts of what would be a worldwide revolutionary movement.

One of the most influential of the leftist government ministers was José Vasconcelos, who as Minister of Education launched major programs to build rural schools, promote traditional Mexican crafts, and underwrite the arts. Vasconcelos was a social democrat and visionary who spoke of Mexicans as being "una raza cosmica," a cosmic, or mixed, race made up of elements of all races, but especially the mixture between Indians and the Spanish conquerors. In place of the scorn heaped on Mexican

José Guadalupe Posada, calavera etching entitled Calaveras del Monton.

NÚMERO 1.
CALAVERAS DEL MONTON.

Es la vida pasajera
Y todos pelan el diente,
Aquí está la calavera,
Del que ha sido presidente.
También la de Don Ramón
Y todos sus subalternos
Son como buenos Gobiernos
Calaveras del montón.

No cavea ya en el Panteón
Es mucha la guesamenta,
Entre ellas también se cuenta:
La de Linda y Escandóu,
Que les prendan sus siriales
A nombre de la Nación
Alcabo que son iguales;
Calaveras del montón.

Las otras son de Oficiales
Sin ninguna distinción,
Coroneles. . . . . Generales
Y jefes de división
Mayores con charreteras
Capitanes de instrucción,
Toditos son calaveras
Calaveras del montón.

A la vez los ayudantes
Con todito su Escuadrón.
Y siguen los Aspirantes:
Calaveras todos son.
Calavera es el Teniente
Y también la reclusión,
Y lo mismo el subteniente
Calaveras del montón.

Esto si que es un recreo
Nadie de morir se escapa
A las muertes con su capa
Diciendo misa las veo,
Y responsos para el Papa.
Ya le prendieron sus ceras
Y se hayan en oración
Calaveras del montón.

También al fuereño toca
Su partesita en la fiesta,
Que por abrir la boca:
Un eléctrico lo acuesta.
El andar en la función,
Toditos son calaveras
Calaveras del montón.

Muchos hicieron corajes
Y sucumbieron de enojo,
Fueron grandes personajes:
E hicieron todo á su antojo.
Como fieles y constantes
De su patria en la Nación;
Calaveras todos son.

Empesamos por el chino
Y vamos viendo despues,
Que al llegar á su destino:
Murió con el Japones.
La china fué la primera
Un representante envió,
Y se quedó calavera;
De tantas cosas que vió.

España un enviado dió
Que fué especial y muy fiel,
Pues al momento cumplió,
Con el encargo del Rey.
Tu persona placentera
Va en mi representación,
Pero quedó calavera
Calavera del montón.

Los valientes tiradores,
Soldados de artillería
Juntos con los zapadores;
Calaveras son en este dia
El soldado de primera
Y el cabo de pelotón;
Con su horrible calavera
Espantan en el panteón.

Calaveras por millares
Se van contando por cientos,
Todos fueron militares;
Y pasaron por sargentos
Comandantes de sección
Que se numere la hilera
Que grita la calavera:
Ya estamos en el panteón.

Ya se llenó el panteón
No queda ni un ahujero,
Pues se cuentan por montón;
Calaveras por entero.
Hoy el sepulturero
Escarba como una fiera,
Y busca la calavera;
De Don Francisco Madero.

Que de pezar se murió
Sin encontrar á la suerte;
La muerte se lo llevó
En su lomo como fuerte.
Madero murió inosente
Pero quedó en la madera
Por querer ser presidente
Lo volvieron calavera.

Todo charlatán pulquero
Que á mujeres engañó,
Calavera se volvió;
Tan solo por embustero.
Aquél que vendió su quezo
Con la muerte allá en la plaza,
Se ha quedado como tiezo
Calavera de su casa.

El vendedor de las peras
Los saca muelas chorriados,
Se han quedado calaveras;
Y con los dientes pelados.
Y aquellos que se murieron
Enfermos del corazón,
Ya sus velas les prendieron;
Calaveras del montón.

Ya las inditas placeras
No hicieron buena fortuna,
Por andar vendiendo tuna;
Se volvieron calaveras.
Lo mismo el del chicharrón
Y todas las euchiladeras;
Son roídas calaveras;
Calaveras del montón.

Imprenta de Antonio Vanegas Arroyo.—2ª Calle de Santa Teresa, Número 43.—México año de 1910.

Indians by the *científicos*, Vasconcelos developed an ideology that lionized Mexico's Indian past. His popular reforms, many felt (particularly students and artists), were much like a national rebirth. Because the arts were seen as a means to inspire and effect social change, artists, writers, composers, and dancers were encouraged to develop themes that would express this vision. "Idealists, persist in the salvation of the Republic," one professor appealed to his students. "Turn your eyes to the soil of Mexico, to our customs and our traditions, our hopes and our wishes, to what we in truth are!"

At the time this ideology was being worked out, Frida was beginning her secondary education. For a while, she attended the local school in Coyoacán, but her father didn't think it was challenging enough for her. The family looked at Mexico City's German school, but Guillermo, who was an atheist, didn't like its religious curriculum. Finally, the choice was made to send her to what was probably the nation's best high school, the National Preparatory School, a model secondary school that was secular, run by the national government—and best of all for the still financially strapped Kahlos—free.

For Frida school was a liberating force. It got her out of Coyoacán, which at the time she complained was boring ("Indians and Indians, and huts and huts . . . so that I am very bored with a *b* of burro," she wrote in one letter), and thrust her into the middle of post-revolutionary life, where modern Mexico was being invented—and where the students were not only vital and major participants in, but leading, that invention—at the center of Mexico City.[8]

The school was located several blocks from the Zócalo, the main plaza that lay at the ancient heart of the city and which had been the central ceremonial plaza of Tenochtitlán, as Mexico City was called before the Spanish conquest. The Spanish leveled the more than seventy Aztec temples, schools, and palaces that had been built around this plaza and built their own symbols of power—the National Cathedral and the National Palace. The National Preparatory School was a slightly later Spanish addition. Of baroque design, it was constructed in 1740 as a Jesuit school and was opened as a secular, government school in 1910, just before the start of the Revolution.

In 1922, Frida's first year at the Preparatoria, she was one of only thirty-five girls enrolled in a student body of two thousand. On enrollment, the students were required to choose a curriculum that would lead to university studies and entrance into one of the professions. Frida decided she wanted to become a doctor and chose courses that would eventually take her to medical school.

Her friends from those days recall a slender and striking young woman who stood out from the other girls. Although the school required no uniform, Frida often wore German-style student garb: a dark blue pleated skirt, socks, boots, and a straw hat with ribbons hanging down the back. She still walked with a slight limp, but if anything this made her more exotic. By now, she had learned how to cope with her limp and the taunts she had received as a child. She used her innate powers of observation, heightened during her childhood illness, to figure people and played her weaknesses as strengths, projecting her eccentricities as mysteries.

Frida quickly befriended students in several cliques at the school. In the morning she might enjoy time before classes with the Contemporáneos, an advant-garde literary group of students, several of whom would later become well-known poets and critics. At lunch, she often talked with some of the Maistros, who were fiery supporters of Vasconcelos. However, the group she liked the most, and which accepted her wholeheartedly, was the Cachuchas (the Spanish name for the caps they wore), the school's most ambitious and rebellious students.

There were nine in this group—seven boys and two girls—all of whom went on to become exceptional members of Mexico's professional class. They were politically aware, although not necessarily politically involved, and identified themselves as being of the left, even though they shunned politicians of all stripes (they thought them short-sighted and self-serving). Rather, they embraced a kind of romantic socialism mixed with high ideals for their own and their country's future. But their most distinguishing features were an irreverence for almost everything and a prankish, anarchistic sensibility. It was this insouciance, innocent at heart, which attracted Frida toward them. "The joking attitude we had toward people drew Frida toward us," one of them later recalled. "Not because she had the habit of laughing at other people but because it captivated her, and she began to learn it, and ended by becoming a master at puns and, when they were called for, of cutting witticism."[9]

Although Frida was a good student, she wasn't a dedicated one. She often cut classes with other Cachuchas to hang out in the streets and public gardens of the nearby university district. Frida, Agustina Reyes, and Carmen Jaime, her closest female friends at school, passed time playing games at streetside arcades and listening to itinerant musicians. Another favorite hangout, and the Cachucha's meeting place, was the Ibero American Library. But it was in the streets that Frida picked up the slang that she liked to use throughout her life, especially to shock unsuspecting society matrons.

When Frida came to the Escuela Preparatoria in 1922, undoubtably one of the first things to arouse her curiosity was a mural that was being painted in the school's auditorium. Minister of Education Vasconcelos used various parts of the school as a place to try out new talent for an ambitious national mural program that he had conceived. Vasconcelos had given the wall behind the stage to the artist Diego Rivera, who had only just returned to his native country after a fourteen-year sojourn in Europe.

Rivera had assembled a small team of dedicated artists and artisans to help him with the project, called *Creation*, which was to take up 150 square meters of wall space. Scaffolding was erected, and worktables were set up to mix plaster, pigments, beeswax, and resin for the encaustic technique Rivera would employ. Rivera and his assistants gridded out the space and drew scenes on the walls with charcoal. At the center was a female figure, clad in goatskin and blowing golden pipes, representing the muse of music. She is flanked on left and right by three male and four female figures who represent respectively the Christian virtues of Faith, Hope, and Charity and Prudence, Justice, Continence, and Strength. The model for the central figure was Rivera's new wife, Lupe Marín, who would spend most days helping her husband with his work at the school.

Rivera was a vivant and ladies man who liked to talk while he worked. He also cut an unforgettable figure. Hugely fat, with an enormous potbelly, protruding eyes, and a sly smile, he looked like a cross between a lecherous Buddha and an anthropomorphized pre-Columbian deity—a Frog Prince—an endearment Frida would use for him later in her life. But at that time, Frida and her friends simply called him *panzón*, "fat belly."

One of the central myths of the Frida Kahlo legend concerns Frida's supposed immediate attraction to Rivera, which includes a conversation with her friends in which she said, "My ambition is to have a child by Diego Rivera. And I'm going to tell him so someday."[10] In his biography, Rivera, a notorious fabulist, recalled the first time that Frida caught his attention:

One night as I was painting high on the scaffold and Lupe [Marín, Rivera's wife] was weaving below, there was a loud shouting and pushing against the auditorium door. All of a sudden the door flew open and a girl who seemed to be no more than ten or twelve was propelled inside. . . .

She was dressed like any other high school student but her manner immediately set her apart. She had unusual dignity and self-assurance, and there was a strange fire in her eyes. . . .

She looked straight up at me. "Would it cause you any annoyance if I watched you at work?" she asked.

"No, young lady, I'd be charmed," I said.

She sat down and watched me silently, her eyes riveted on every move of my paintbrush. After a few hours, Lupe's jealousy was enraged and she began to insult the girl. . . . The girl merely stiffened and returned Lupe's stare without a word.[11]

Both of these recollections were made years later and benefit from hindsight, and in Rivera's case, from much imaginative embellishment. It is more likely that Frida did have some sort of unfocused fascination with Rivera (he was unforgettable) and that Rivera, who always had an eye for pretty young women, noticed, then forgot, this particular one—that is, until he was prompted to "remember" her when she made a much more vivid impression on him six years later.

Other events at the Preparatoria were likely to have taken Rivera's attention away from Frida. At the time he was painting *Creation*, a battle over the theme of Vasconcelos's mural project had been joined. In the Preparatoria, an active clique of ultra-conservative students from some of the wealthier families violently protested the work of Diego Rivera and other muralists. This group began attacking Rivera verbally—accusing him of propagating atheism and socialism—then defaced murals painted by the artists José Clemente Orozco and David Alfaro Siquieros in the school's courtyard. Rivera responded by getting a few of his friends to act as guards of his work (which in any event was well-protected behind the locked doors of the auditorium) and, along with the other painters, by wearing pistols while they were painting. The pistol-waving artist was a role that he developed with gusto—perhaps as a way to compensate for the fact that he had conveniently missed action in the Mexican Revolution.

From Frida's perspective, Rivera, the revolutionary gunman, can only have added greater allure to his already oversized persona. Nonetheless, in the school year 1922–23, Frida was still just fifteen, and in spite of her play of sophistication and poise, was more of a child than she wanted to admit. Rivera was thirty-six and living in a world far removed from her own. More important, Frida had developed a serious crush on one of her fellow students. Within a few months she would forget about *panzón* and focus her attentions elsewhere.

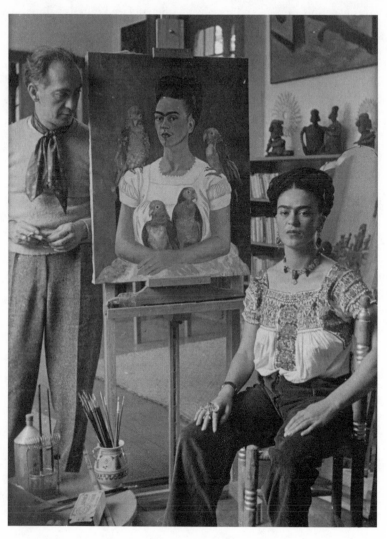

Frida painting Me and My Parrots as Nickolas Muray watches.
(Studio in the Blue House, 1941)

3

The Ballerina

Who was Frida Kahlo? There's no way to answer this exactly.
Her personality was so contradictory that you could say there
were many Fridas. Maybe none the one she wanted to be.

—*Alejandro Gómez Arias*

THE LEADER OF THE CACHUCHAS was a young man named Alejandro Gómez Arias. Smart, disciplined, eloquent, Gómez Arias would later become a well-known lawyer and journalist. At the Preparatoria, he already possessed many of the qualities that would mark him as one of Mexico's leading intellectuals. He was serious, yet ironic, an enemy of double-talking politicians and defenders of the status quo. A Mexican nationalist and socialist—and an idealist with impossibly high expectations for himself, his friends, and his country—he believed that he and the other Cachuchas could help lead Mexico into a new, more enlightened era. "Optimism, sacrifice, purity, love, joy are the orator's social mission," he would tell his friends. Revolution was still in the air and a future of enlightened social change seemed possible for those bold enough to reach for it.

Like Frida, Gómez Arias read constantly and broadly: Spengler, Hegel, Kant, Pushkin, Golgol, Tolstoy, topical political tracts, Mexican novels old and new, especially the great novel of the Mexican Revolution, *The Underdogs* by Mariano Azuela. Gómez Arias and Frida began to spend long hours together in the Ibero American Library, which was located only a few blocks from the National Preparatory School. By the summer of 1923, they had fallen in love. Their relationship is interesting because it offers a view of Frida's personality through her tempestuous letters, and because her courtship with Gómez Arias foreshadows her relationships with other men later in her life.

One trait that Frida displayed immediately was her choice of lovers. There were seven young men in the Cachuchas, one a poet and scholar of Chinese poetry, others writers and soon-to-be lawyers, doctors, and journalists. All were witty, vibrant, full of life. But the one Frida wooed was the leader, the most outstanding of the group. Choosing men with strong personalities, men who could bring attention to her by virtue of her union with them, was a habit she would continue throughout her life.

From descriptions by the other Cachuchas, Gómez Arias comes off as a brilliant young man, a charismatic orator, but reserved and aloof, not the kind to fall head over heels in love. Undoubtably there must have been a mutual dance of attraction and testing between them, with Frida employing all of her considerable skills of charm and intelligence to make him notice her. Yet, in spite of this nuanced assertiveness, at the beginning of their love affair, she could hardly believe that he saw something special in her. This nagging and veiled feeling of unworthiness would always haunt her. "Alex," she wrote him in August 1923,

> I received your note yesterday at seven in the evening when I least expected that someone would remember me, and least of all Dr. Alejandro, but luckily I was mistaken. . . . You don't know how delighted I was that you had confidence in me as if I were a true friend and you spoke to me as you had never spoken before, since you tell me with little irony that I am so superior and I am so far beyond you, I will see the basis of those lines and not see what others would see in them. . . .

[I]f good intentions are enough for you not only is my hum-
ble advice yours but all of me is yours. . . .

Well, Alex, write to me often and long, the longer the
better, and meanwhile receive all the love of

Frieda[1]

A brief revolt flared up in late November 1923 against the
Obregón government. By December, fighting had moved near
to Mexico City, and Matilde Kahlo kept her headstrong daughter at home in Coyoacán, causing Frida intense anguish at not
being able to see Gómez Arias. On New Year's Day 1924, Frida
wrote Alejandro wishing him safety. Despite claims she later
made about becoming a religious skeptic early in life, this letter
shows her at sixteen still to be a conventional Catholic schoolgirl. "My Alex, . . . Where did you spend New Year's Eve? I went
to the Campos' house and it was as usual since we spent the
whole time praying and afterward because I was so sleepy I went
to sleep and did not dance at all. This morning I took communion and prayed to God for all of you."

In a letter from April that year when she went on a religious
retreat, Frida wrote Alejandro about her feelings during this
period of contemplation:

The exercises of the retreat were beautiful because the priest
that directed them was very intelligent and almost a saint. In
the general communion they gave us the papal benediction and
one gains many indulgences and one can ask for as many as you
want. . . . I . . . prayed to God and to the Virgin that everything
should go well for you and that you should love me always.[2]

Sometime in 1924, probably in the fall when they both were
seeing each other daily at school, they moved from being sweet-

hearts to lovers. Gómez Arias, who of all of Frida's acquaintances, including Diego Rivera, made the most astute observations about her, was impressed with her ease and lack of inhibitions in making love. "Frida was sexually precocious," he remembered later in life. "To her, sex was a form of enjoying life, a kind of vital impulse." Nonetheless, for a woman of Frida's class having sexual relations that young and before marriage was considered a scandalous violation of socially accepted norms. On Christmas Day 1924, she wrote Gómez Arias a letter that reflects not only their newfound physical intimacy but a sense of insecurity that haunted her for having broken this taboo. "My Alex,"

> Since I saw you I have loved you. Because it will probably be a few days before we see each other, I am going to beg you not to forget your pretty woman. . . . sometimes at night I am very afraid and I would like you to be with me so that I should be less frightened and so that you can tell me that you love me as much as before; as much as last December, even if I am an "easy thing" right Alex? You must keep on liking easy things.[3]

In January 1925, Frida began looking for work that she could fit around her school schedule. Because her father's business was still shaky, her income was important to her family. She took a course in typing, worked as a cashier in a pharmacy, and even held down a factory job for a few weeks. But the job that interested her most was the apprentice position she took with Fernando Fernández, a commercial printer who was a friend of her father's. Fernández saw that she had talent as an artist and gave her exercises copying the drawings of Swedish impressionist Anders Zorn. This recognition of her talent was important to Frida, even though the idea of becoming a full-time artist hadn't occurred to her yet. (Years later she would frame a letter from Fernández commending her work and hang it in her studio in the Blue House.)

In early 1925, Alejandro began to give Frida signs that he wanted out of their relationship, or at the least, that he wanted to alter its terms. Over the next seven to eight months, slowly—and very much against Frida's wishes—they reverted to a chaste arrangement, friends rather than lovers. Frida anguished over this breakup even as she indulged herself with two brief affairs, one with her mentor Fernández, and at around the same time another with a female librarian at the Ministry of Education library (apparently Frida's first lesbian encounter) where Frida had gone to apply for a job.

As part of their campaign against bourgeois respectability, Frida and Alejandro had agreed that their sexual friendship should not bind them exclusively to one another. They also talked with each other about their dalliances with other lovers. But when Frida told Gómez Arias about her trysts, he spoiled his revolutionary credentials by bad-mouthing her to their Cachucha friends. When she learned of this, she wrote to him a letter full of hurt and dismay:

> I went around with Agustina Reyna all day, according to what she says, she no longer wants to be with me much, because you told her that she was the same or worse than me, and that is a great disparagement for her. . . .
>
> She says that on various occasions you told her some of the things that I told you, details that I never told Reyna . . . The fact is that now no one wants to be my friend because I have lost my reputation, something that I cannot remedy. I will have to be friends with those who like me the way I am.

In spite of Alejandro's dwindling ardor, Frida clung to the hope that somehow they would reconcile their differences and rekindle their special bond. "For nothing in this life can I stop talking to you," she wrote him. "I will not be your *novia*, but I will always talk to you even if you do not answer me . . . because I love you more than ever, now that you are preparing to leave me."[4]

It was during this time when her first serious relationship was ending that Frida suffered a grievous injury that would irrevocably alter the course of her life. It happened late in the afternoon of September 17, 1925, in downtown Mexico City only a few blocks from the Zócalo and the National Preparatory School. She and Alejandro Gómez Arias were traveling together on a bus that was to take her back to Coyoacán. As the bus began to turn a corner it was hit by a slow-moving electric trolley. At first, it seemed as if this were a caricature or hallucination of an accident, as though two ponderous, inflated toys were jostling each other in some harmless game. But mysteriously the trolley didn't stop. Instead it pushed the bus against a wall in front of the busy San Juan market.

> The bus had a strange elasticity. It bent more and more, but for a time it did not break. It was a bus with long benches on either side. I remember that at one moment my knees touched the knees of the person sitting opposite me. . . . When the bus reached it's maximum flexibility it burst into a thousand pieces, and the train kept moving. It ran over many people.

The bus's disintegration threw Gómez Arias under the tracks of the trolley. It's three cars passed over him; miraculously, except for a few cuts and bruises, he was unhurt. After he got up and dusted himself off, he looked around for Frida:

> Something strange had happened. Frida was totally nude. The collision had unfastened her clothes. Someone in the

bus, probably a house painter, had been carrying a packet of powdered gold. This package broke, and the gold fell all over the bleeding body of Frida. When people saw her they cried, "*La bailarina, la bailarina!*" With the gold on her red, bloody body, they thought she was a dancer.[5]

When the bus went to pieces a section of metal handrail snapped; it was driven through Frida's hip and came out the other side of her body through her vagina. In the panic and confusion, a bystander insisted that the metal shaft should be pulled out. Gómez Arias consented and the man put his knee to Frida's back and yanked out the spear that had impaled her. Alejandro gently picked her up and placed her on a billiard table of a nearby pool hall. He covered her with his coat and waited with her. Several other passengers had been killed immediately and many others were as seriously injured as Frida. He expected her to die before the ambulance reached them. When the piece of iron was pulled out of her body, Frida screamed so loud that in Gómez Arias's words, "when the ambulance arrived . . . her screaming was louder than the siren."

But she had been, to some degree, lucky. The rod had grazed her spine, cracking several vertebrae, and fractured her pelvis. She also suffered broken ribs, multiple fractures of her right leg, and a crushed right foot. Yet no major blood vessels had been cut, which saved her life.

Frida was taken to the Red Cross Hospital, a dark and dilapidated place housed in an old convent in central Mexico City, where she underwent the first of many operations she would endure in her life. The doctors, in the words of one of her friends, "put her back together in sections as if they were making a photomontage."

The Red Cross Hospital was a charity hospital and the service was basic. Judged by the standards of their day, the physicians who attended her weren't necessarily incompetent. Some of Frida's injuries were so severe there was little that could be done at that time to repair them. With packed wards, the doctors also didn't have time enough to spend with each patient. Because the Kahlos didn't have money for more expensive and expert treatment, they kept Frida there rather than move her to another hospital where she would have received more intensive care.

For several weeks, the doctors concentrated on ridding her of peritonitis, the most immediate threat to her life. They set the breaks in her right leg and did what they could to mend her right foot. To immobilize her, they put her in a full-torso cast and kept her pinned to her bed inside a particularly ominous-looking contraption shaped like a coffin.

Frida stayed at Red Cross for a month. When the danger of death had passed they allowed her to be taken back to Coyoacán and cared for at home, where she convalesced for two more months. By early December she had recovered enough to walk; just before Christmas she made her first trip back into Mexico City, where she waited in vain outside the house of Alejandro Gómez Arias. He never showed up to meet her.

Through the winter and spring of 1926 Frida began to reemerge into the world. She had missed the fall semester at the Preparatoria and didn't bother to register for the spring term either. She may have had plans to finish school in the fall of 1926, but that summer she began experiencing intense shooting pain in her back. A new set of doctors was called in and discovered something that the first set had missed: three spinal fractures. She was put back in bed in a full-torso cast for the rest of the year.

During the summer and fall of 1926, Frida gradually gave up the idea of becoming a doctor, but in a strange alchemy she became something else—a professional patient. Yet, in spite of her ordeals, she hadn't lost what was to become her indomitable will to live. Forced to lie in her bed day after day, she soon discovered a new, intensely interesting way to pass the time. She confiscated a box of paints that belonged to her father and had a carpenter construct a specially designed easel to hold canvas and sketch books she could work on while lying flat on her back in bed. It was then that she she began to paint, seriously, for the first time.

Her first subjects were her sister Adriana, friends from the neighborhood, and fellow Cachuchas, but her best and most intensely felt painting from 1926–27 was the first one she worked on, a portrait of herself. Beginning a habit she would carry throughout her life, Frida chose a recipient for this painting before she had applied the first stroke. The work, in which she is wearing a dark red velvet dress with a plunging neckline that reveals ivory-colored skin, was a gift to Alejandro Gómez Arias. She painted her right hand held open as though indicating her wish for reconciliation with her former lover. The entire work is a coded sign of longing and need, yet there is also an overt note of self-reliance that protects her from seeming too dependent. At the bottom of the painting she wrote in German, *Heute ist Immer Noch*—Today still goes on.

Frida called her likeness in the painting "Botticeli," (misspelling the painter's name; she never bothered with minor annoyances like proper spelling). In April 1927, when Gómez Arias had just begun a six-month tour of Europe, she wrote him, "Your Botticeli is well, but underneath it all one sees in her a certain sadness that she naturally cannot disguise." She also wrote him long letters in which she described her painful daily routines to him in great detail, ending one by saying, "How much I would like to explain my suffering to you minute by minute."

There can be no denying that her physical pain was real and her condition must have been terribly depressing. Yet Frida also knew how to invoke pain and suffering to attain the maximum effects of guilt and pity on her beloved. She had identified Alejandro Gómez Arias as a man of destiny and was still using every means possible to make him hers.

All of Frida's friends in Mexico have said that this dreadful accident changed her. The Frida Kahlo of 1927 and after was a sadder person than her prankish alter ego before the wreck. Unsurprisingly, she was also much more given to personal introspection, although she didn't share her insights with most of her friends.

Like the ill six-year-old she had been, the one with the imaginary playmate she could find by crawling through the "O" in "Pinzón," she divided herself into two faces she offered the world. One was full of alegría, the devil-may-care Frida. According to Adelina Zendejas, one of her school friends, "When we went to visit her when she was sick, she played, she laughed, she commented, she made caustic criticisms, witticisms, and wise opinions. If she cried, no one knew it." Yet to Alejandro Gómez Arias, and probably only to him at this time, Frida revealed another, bleaker side. "Why do you study so much?" she asked him,

> What secret are you looking for? Life will soon reveal itself to you. I already know everything, without reading or writing. A short while ago, maybe a few days ago, I was a girl walking in a world of colors, of clear and tangible shapes. Everything was mysterious and something was hiding. Guessing its nature was a game for me. If you knew how terrible it is to attain knowledge all of a sudden—like lightning elucidating the earth! Now I live in a painful planet, transparent as ice. It's as if I learned everything at the same time, in a matter of seconds. My girlfriends and my companions slowly became women. I grew up in a few instants and now everything is dull and flat. I know there is nothing behind; if there were something I would see it.[6]

In spite of her sadness and introspection, in some important ways Frida hadn't changed at all. Out of this crisis year of 1925 came an intensification of something that was already well-developed in her. She began to learn how to cultivate and use a mythology of personal suffering—as a deep expression of her spiritual longing—and as a mechanism for personal aggrandizement. The former is something that is usually acknowledged as a virtue; the latter, a noxious alloy of emotional manipulation, cunning foresight, personal insecurity, and craven neediness, is handled with considerably more wariness. In Frida Kahlo these two parts merged into a complex psychological whole, one that is not easy to separate. It animated her personality and made her fascinating to many who met her. In time the originality of her developing persona would attract and enchant Mexico's leading artist, another strong and successful man. He and Frida would begin a journey together that has become legendary for its intensity and its contradictions.

Frida and Diego Rivera, San Francisco, 1930.

4

Mexican Dionysus

I have suffered two great accidents in my life. One in which a streetcar knocked me down. . . . The other accident is Diego.

—*Frida Kahlo*

BY THE END OF 1927, Frida had emerged from her cocoon of orthopedic corsets into the world of arts and politics in Mexico City. She had decided not to finish her course work at the Preparatoria; instead she would be an artist, for which a diploma was unnecessary. She was as yet unsure about the direction her art would take. She felt she had a talent for portraiture, but she was aware enough of the currents in European and Mexican art to know that portraiture was a beginning, not an end, for her. In the meanwhile, she renewed old friendships in her network of friends from the Preparatoria—most of them now university students—opening a pathway for her life and art.

In the months of her recuperation, as her relationship with Alejandro Gómez Arias had withered she had deepened her friendship with Germán de Campo, who had been a member of the Maistros clique at the National Preparatory School. De Campo was now enrolled at the law school of the National University and was still a passionate supporter of former education minister José Vasconcelos, who in 1928 had embarked on what would prove to be an unsuccessful campaign for the Mexican presidency.

The Vasconcelos campaign was only one thread in a web of protest groups to which de Campo belonged. Others included the Communist-directed Anti-Imperialist League, which published a paper and organized demonstrations against United States intervention in the Americas and European colonial policy in Africa and Asia, and the National Student Confederation, which agitated for the right of students at the National University to have greater independence from the government in the selection of courses and hiring of teachers.

Early in 1928, as Frida made the rounds of leftist parties and organizing committee meetings with Germán de Campo, she met an intriguing circle of artists and revolutionaries based around Tina Modotti, an American who had come to live in Mexico City in 1923. Modotti had begun her stay in Mexico as the lover and apprentice of American photographer Edward Weston, but had remained in Mexico after Weston left the country in 1924. She was a beautiful woman, earthy and ethereal at the same time, who had talent as a photographer and lived an unconventional life. She had also developed into a mainstay of the then-fledgling Mexican Communist party, acting as translator, writer, and photographer for its newspaper, *El Machete*. She was a perfect role model for twenty-one-year-old Frida Kahlo, and the two women soon became friends.

Modotti was only one of a small, but influential circle of Americans who had come to Mexico during the late teens and twenties seeking refuge from military service and the headlong rush of American material culture. The first wave of American exiles included the so-called "slackers," pacifists and leftists evading the draft that the U.S. government had enacted to fill army ranks after the United States entered World War I. This bunch included the writer Carleton Beals and writer and Communist activist Bertram Wolfe. Wolfe, who was on the run from a federal indictment issued during the Red Scare in the early 1920s, actually ran the Mexican Communist party for a while as an agent of the Communist International, or Comintern, based in Moscow. During his stint as Comintern agent, he got to know Diego Rivera, then a party member. He would later become a close friend of Frida as well.

Other Americans included the writers Frances Toor, who founded the magazine *Mexican Folkways* in 1925 to tell Americans about Mexico and Mexican culture, and Anita Brenner, who would write the best-selling book about Mexico, *Idols Behind Altars*, in 1929. The writers Katherine Anne Porter and John Dos Passos stayed, separately, in Mexico at various times during the 1920s, and in 1931 Mexico offered its hospitality to the poet Hart Crane, who praised it as a place of "simple courtesies, and constant sunlight—it enthralls me more than any spot on earth I've ever known. It is and isn't an easy place to live. Altogether more strange to us than the orient. . . . There is never an end to dancing, singing, rockets, and the rather lurking and suave danger that gives the same edge to life here that the mountains give to the horizon. Thank God some new sensation to encounter—something less sterile than U.S. robotization."[1]

The theme that Mexico was in Crane's phrase, "another world," one of simple, unmechanized pleasures, would echo throughout much of the American expatriate community. Their Mexico was, as Carleton Beals wrote, a country in which "a Mexican peasant's life is one texture. Work is pleasure; and pleasure is work. The day for him is woven into a unity, satisfying in its completeness." That this work of "unity" and "pleasure" also included back-breaking toil for poverty-level wages apparently never bothered Beals, Crane, or the other American romanticizers. Frida, whose knowledge of Mexico was more immediate and generally less sentimental, did not wholly subscribe to this view of her country, although she did tend to see the Indians and Mexican peasantry through the same rosy light.

Contrary to her fable that she joined the Young Communist League at thirteen during the last days of the Mexican Revolution, Frida almost certainly began her Communist affiliation sometime during 1928 or 1929.

In his memoirs written toward the end of his life, Bertram Wolfe captured part of communism's appeal at that time. It

> derived in part from the fact that it was an untried ideal and that it was learnedly pronounced. It was clever of Marx to . . . avoid as "unscientific" any attempt to picture the future society that was to replace the one he was criticizing. . . . For me, as for most sensitive persons, the existing society had many obvious defects, imperfections, things that could be improved, shortcomings from our dreams of perfection. . . . How nice to think that one had answers to all problems, cures for all ills, a simple, certain, manifest remedy backed by books of enormous learning.[2]

In his introduction to the published version of the notebook or journal that Frida kept toward the end of her life, the Mexican writer Carlos Fuentes speculates that "Latin American Communists are really lapsed Catholics in need of reassurance. Having lost the Catholic roof, they yearn for the Communist shelter."[3] Fuentes further notes an observation made by Czech writer Milan Kundera that communism's main appeal to young people is not its critique of capitalism or rational, godless, materialist philosophy, but its seductive dream of purity, its promise of a return to a unity that is so appealing to modern humankind because it is the antithesis of our restless, grasping, fragmented societies.

For Frida, communism almost certainly acted as a replacement for her rather strong Catholic faith (that she had been deeply attached to Catholic tenets is clearly signaled by the vehemence with which she dismissed religion after her switch to communism). What could have been a better replica of the Church than the Party, which paid the Church the ultimate compliment by uncannily adopting its rigid, stratified hierarchy; its intolerant certitudes; its inquisitorial purges; and its all-powerful head, the Party secretary (during most of Frida's life, the ruthless dictator Joseph Stalin).

During Frida's youth, the mid-1920s through the mid-1930s, it was de rigueur for an aspiring artist to embrace either communism or Surrealism or both. To be reactionary, or even middle of the road, and be considered an important artist was out of the question. Only a few tough contrarians—José Clemente Orozco in Mexico, Thomas Hart Benton in the United States, to name two—managed to resist this intense form of peer pressure. If one were young and ambitious, it was wise to at least mouth the pieties of social revolution and Surrealist dreamscape.

There is absolutely no sign that Frida was insincerely playing the part of daring, young revolutionary. Her energetic personality, questioning of authority, and her love for the culture of the streets, tilted her toward a sincere embrace of the Communist worldview. In Mexico, a young progressive's enemies were clearly visible. They were found in the dead hand of the authoritarian, archconservative Church; the veiled machinations of the land-holding elites, who despite the Revolution still clung to considerable power; and the arrogant and assertive thrust of U.S. political and economic power in Mexico and other countries of the region.

There was also another enemy that was far more elusive than the almost cardboard characters of the manipulative priest and the bustling American capitalist. This was the Mexican regime itself, which proclaimed itself the very embodiment of the Mexican Revolution. Yet this very same political presence was deeply suspect in the eyes of Mexican leftists.

During the twenties, presidents Alvaro Obregón and Plutarco Calles deferred to the U.S government in regard to the still considerable American holdings in Mexico. The compromises made by successive Mexican governments provided grist for Mexican leftists and irritated the Mexican psyche, which had not yet come to terms with the battering it had taken from the United States, Britain, and France in the nineteenth century, and by American intervention in the Mexican Revolution during the teens. Yet this same regime was the first in Mexican history to promote the idea that Mexicans were exceptional, a people who were neither wholly European, nor Indian, but a mix whose abilities, imagination, and vital force should be recognized and celebrated. Mexican leftists, who were also Mexican nationalists, favored this position, and it left them in a perpetual quandary about what attitude to strike toward their own government.

Thus it was that Frida, taken by the glamour and excitement of Tina Modotti's world, and excited by the prospect of being part of a movement to achieve utopian social change, joined the Communist party. She became a regular at the parties that Modotti held at her house. These events were high-spirited and included a mix of Americans and Mexicans of the left and visiting artists of various, usually unidentifiable political stripes. Art, politics, and gossip mingled into one long, boozy conversation as guests flirted, fought, and argued over Surrealism, the role of the Communist party in fostering revolution in Mexico, the place of nationalism in art and politics, and the individual worth of other partygoers.

At one of these get-togethers in 1928 Frida became reacquainted with old *panzón*, fat belly, Diego Rivera, the man who had briefly fascinated her during her first year at the Preparatoria in 1922. She remembered her first meeting with Rivera at Tina Modotti's house:

took place in the period when people carried pistols and went around shooting the street lamps on Madero Avenue and getting into mischief. During the night, they broke them all and went about spraying bullets, just for fun. Once at a party, given by Tina, Diego shot a phonograph and I began to be very interested in him in spite of the fear I had of him.[4]

Rivera in 1928 had just become an international celebrity. Only months before, he had returned from Moscow where he had conferred with Russian Communist officials and had at first been treated like a visiting dignitary. However, toward the end of his trip, when he had sided with a group of artists that was on the outs with the Soviet bureaucracy, Rivera had been asked to return to Mexico "to assist the Mexican Communist party's presidential campaign," a euphemism for expulsion from the country. Typically, Rivera embroidered a tale that transformed him into a hero of Soviet art and recast his return to Mexico as a triumph.

Recently divorced from his second wife, Lupe Marín, Rivera, not surprisingly, was feeling quite sprightly. Yet for an aspiring Don Juan with a mammoth passion for beauty, he was not altogether an appealing package himself. He was still gigantically fat, perhaps suffered from health problems, maybe even periodic impotence. Furthermore, according to Lupe Marín, he hardly ever bathed. Thus we must imagine at Tina Modotti's party a filthy as well as gross Diego Rivera, fable-spinning nonstop about the most fantastic events—that he was briefly a cannibal during his art school days, for instance—bluffing and boasting, shooting out street lights and offending songs on the phonograph, and weaving a web of dubious enchantment out of stories that most people knew were pure nonsense.

Furthermore, although this wasn't considered exceptional in Mexico in 1928, Rivera, was the living embodiment of Mexican

Fading Light: The Tragedy of Tina Modotti

In the 1920s, Mexico City was a near rival to Paris and New York for the glamour of its arts and danger of its political intrigue. Like Paris (and unlike New York at that time), Mexico City was a cheap place to live. Also, unlike either Paris or New York, it seemed to dazzle with new possibilities and revolutionary potential. For leftists and left sympathizers, especially those in the arts, it was an immensely attractive city, second only to Moscow as a place that might become a capital of world revolution. And unlike Moscow it never snowed or had dreary winters. It offered an ideal destination for expatriate artists who sought adventure and cultural space to express themselves in their art. During these heady days, no talent and personality shone brighter than Tina Modotti.

A daughter of the Italian working class, Modotti immigrated to the United States when she was seventeen, joining her sister and father in San Francisco. She had a brief career as an actress in the Italian theater of San Francisco before moving to Los Angeles to seek work in silent films.

In 1920 she landed her first and only major role, as a Mexican temptress in *The Tiger's Coat*. She followed this up in 1921 with bit parts in a western, *Riding with Death*, a vehicle for cowboy star Charles "Buck" Jones, and *I Can Explain*, a saga of unbridled passion and doomed love. As before, she was typecast as a Latin *femme fatale*. In Los Angeles, Modotti met and modeled for the photographer Edward Weston. They began an affair, and seeking new vistas both struck out for Mexico in 1923.

Modotti and Weston made an immediate impact in Mexico City. They quickly made friends among artists and expatriates, and their apartment in downtown Colonia Juárez became a favored haunt of Mexico City's bohemian and leftist set. But in her own eyes, Modotti's most important achievement during her seven years in Mexico was her growing reputation as a photographer.

Early in her stay, Modotti split with Weston, who returned to Los Angeles to pursue his career. Rebelling against Weston's more conservative, formal aesthetic approach to photography, Modotti immersed herself in radical politics and used her creative talents to help various leftist projects, most notably the Mexican Communist party and its paper *El Machete*. Her shots of the lives of poor Mexicans mark the high point of her photographic career and creative life.

In 1929, Modotti was caught up in a murder which turned into a scandal that ended her Mexican idyll. Ironically, the Mexican press, which painted her as loose and immoral, cast her in the same role tried by Hollywood. On February 5, 1930, she was declared a security risk and deported from the country.

For the next six years Modotti lived in exile in Germany, the Soviet Union, and France. In Moscow, discouraged by an official Soviet orthodoxy that was distrustful of individual artistic vision outside the control of the Party, she left her photography behind, and became a Party militant and began living with Vittorio Vidali, an Italian-born Communist agent she had known in Mexico.

In 1936, Vidali and Modotti were sent by the Comintern to Spain to support the foundering Republican forces in their conflict with Franco's Nationalists. But in February 1939, as the Republican army evaporated in the face of the final Nationalist offensive, Modotti and Vidali fled Spain. In an odd twist of fate, they ended up again in Mexico, which opened its arms to thousands of Spanish refugees. Modotti, still persona non grata in Mexico, was forced to enter Mexico under an assumed name. Tired and drawn, she had suddenly become an old woman at forty-two. She and Vidali took a small apartment in a working-class neighborhood, and she began a thankless and poorly paid job as translator for a Communist labor leader.

Modotti had become a ghost in a country that had nurtured her talent, and she had become an entirely different person from the free-spirited young woman who had taken Mexico by storm in the twenties.

Left: Frida in Tehuana gear and Diego on the roof of their studio/house, San Angel, Mexico, 1939.

Below: Diego Rivera and Frida at a street protest against U.S. intervention in Guatemala. Mexico City, 1953.

With Rosa
Covarrubias
and Nelson A.
Rockefeller in
1939.

At the Cortés Palace in 1931. Left to right: Leo Eloesser, Frida's friend and physician from San Francisco; Frances Flubb Paine, art adviser to the Rockefellers; Frida; Jean Charlot, mural painter; Elie Faure, French critic and Diego Rivera's Paris mentor; Diego Rivera.

machismo. He was a braggart, constantly needing to inflate his ego with fantastic stories about his sexual conquests. He was also insanely jealous of his wives and more serious sexual partners who took other male lovers (he was a major subscriber to sexual double standards for men and women, although he viewed lesbian relations by his lovers as amusing side-events). Many of the visiting American women in Tina Modotti's circle modeled for him and a number of them became his lovers. Even Tina Modotti had only a few years before briefly been his lover. However, by 1928 Modotti was deeply in love with Cuban Communist Julio Antonio Mello and was already beginning to have second thoughts about Rivera. In 1929 she would turn on him completely.

In spite of these deficiencies, it is generally acknowledged that by sheer force of personality Rivera did exert, and with a seemingly natural ease, a powerful attraction on women, especially those in or on the fringes of the art world. He had a prodigal imagination and one of his most compelling attributes was that when he was in the company of most women, he gave them at that moment his undivided attention. He listened, joked, cajoled, sympathized. He was as much a friend as potential lover.

Frida's meeting with Rivera reignited her interest in him. From her viewpoint, Rivera held many attractions. His fame as an artist meant that she might be able to gain recognition for herself through a liaison with him, although this was a long shot (Rivera was self-absorbed and usually didn't go out of his way to help other artists). Certainly his approval of her art meant a lot to her, perhaps too much. She must have felt that if he approved of her and her work, she had worth. This is how unsure she was of herself, not only then, but throughout her relationship with him.

Soon after meeting him, she came to see him with three of her paintings while he was on the scaffolds at the Ministry of Education and asked him his opinion of her work. "If you are interested in them," she said, "tell me so, if not, likewise, so that I will go to work at something else to help my parents." According to Rivera's account in his memoir, *My Art, My Life:*

> They were all three portraits of women. As I looked at them, one by one, I was immediately impressed. The canvases revealed an unusual energy of expression, precise delineation of character, and true severity. They showed none of the tricks in the name of originality that usually mark the work of an ambitious beginner. . . .
>
> "In my opinion, no matter how difficult it is for you, you must continue to paint," I told her.
>
> "Then I'll follow your advice. Now I'd like to ask you one more favor. I've done other paintings which I'd like you to see. Since you don't work on Sundays, could you come by my place next Sunday to see them? I live in Coyoacán, Avenida Londres 126."

Rivera came to see her that Sunday and began seeing her other Sundays as well. Soon she began to come by the Education Ministry building to help him with his work. Fairly quickly, by late 1928 or early 1929, they had begun a romantic and intimate relationship and were in each other's company constantly. Rivera's former wife, Lupe, who was still close to her ex-husband was not amused by the arrival of this young upstart. She complained to Rivera that Frida was uncouth and "drank like a Mariachi."

Rivera paid Frida the compliment of painting her as a revolutionary hero in one of his Ministry of Education panels. In the work, entitled *Insurrection*, Frida, standing in the middle of the fresco, passes out weapons to workers. (Interestingly, Rivera's ex-lover Tina Modotti has been pushed to one side, along with her lover Julio Antonio Mello and future partner Vittorio Vidali, who lurks in the background, looking at Modotti over Mello's shoulder. Unintentionally indicating what a small, almost claustrophobic world they inhabited, on the left side of the panel Rivera painted Modotti's former lover, Xavier Guerrero, as a worker who has just chambered a bullet.)

Rivera was extremely busy during his and Frida's courtship in 1928–29. As soon as he finished the murals at the Ministry of Education, he was given an even grander commission to paint a series of frescoes depicting the sweep of Mexican history from the first cultivation of corn to the present day on the walls of the courtyard of the National Palace, the most prestigious site for frescoes in Mexico. He paused a few months before beginning this to manage the Mexican Communist party's presidential campaign while simultaneously designing the scenes and costumes for the ballet *H.P.* (Horse Power) whose musical score was being written by the renowned Mexican composer Carlos Chávez. On top of that he painted portraits and other canvases in which he reused some of the themes of his frescoes—sending these works to galleries in the United States. He also produced a series of flower paintings and studies of Indian children that were geared for the tourist trade that came to Mexico City.

Rivera painted prodigiously and he had to: he had to support the two children he had with Lupe Marín as well as maintain his increasingly lavish lifestyle (he employed several servants and a chauffeur and he entertained constantly). In short, he was a man who couldn't, and didn't want to, sit still. Frida was just one part of his life, although she was becoming an increasingly important part as the year 1929 progressed.

For her part, buoyed by Diego Rivera's approval, Frida concentrated more than ever on her art. She still painted portraits and self-portraits, but under the sway of Rivera's style—she replaced the somber tones she had used in the self-portrait she had painted for Alejandro Gómez Arias and the portraits of her fellow Cachuchas—with the brighter colors used by Rivera, who had himself appropriated these from the colors found in Mexican folk paintings and on the walls of Mexican taverns and other buildings. She also has dispensed with ornamentation. Her new work used, à la Rivera, fields of color behind the human portrait.

By the spring of 1929, Frida and Rivera found themselves in the middle of ominous political shifts. During the presidential race of 1928, Frida's good friend, Germán de Campo had been assassinated while speaking at a rally for presidential candidate José Vasconcelos. In January 1929 Julio Antonio Mello, a member of the Mexican Communist party's Central Committee, was assassinated by an unidentified gunman. The issue became a scandal when Tina Modotti, was portrayed as a villainess by the more conservative of Mexico City's newspapers. In March, the Mexican government outlawed the Party by declaring it an illegal organization.

Within the Party, Rivera was also being challenged. His decision in April to become director of the San Carlos Academy—his alma mater and the national art school run by the government—was privately criticized by some Party members as a hypocritical alignment with a reactionary regime, as was his continuing fresco work for the government. But more to the point, Rivera's unpredictability and unwillingness to toe the Party line and follow the bureaucratic shifts and Machiavellian intrigues within the Party annoyed some fellow members, especially Vittorio Vidali, who with the departure of Bertram Wolfe was the Comintern's man in Mexico. At some point in 1929 Vidali decided that he had to rid the Party of "undependable" elements—especially Diego Rivera.

Vidali, with the surprising help of Tina Modotti, orchestrated a campaign to expel Rivera from the Party. Obviously, something had gone wrong at the end of Rivera's affair with Modotti, because she began circulating rumors that he was sexually irresponsible, especially toward female Party members, and thus a hindrance to Party discipline. This was an odd accusation for someone with Modotti's own history to make. In the end, Rivera was asked to sign a pledge that his fresco work would not "prevent him from fighting the current reactionary government." He refused and was officially kicked out of the Mexican Communist party in early October 1929.

During the late summer of 1929 Diego Rivera suffered a nervous breakdown as a result of the pressure being exerted on him by his Communist party comrades. For seven years he had aligned himself with the party to the extent that it very nearly identified who he was and how he viewed himself. Of course, he was an artist first and foremost, but an artist whose skill had been placed at the disposal of the class struggle. For Rivera, that struggle was completely contained within the party. And now he was a political outsider.

Trying to regain a foothold on some kind of solid ground, in August he suddenly announced his engagement to Frida Kahlo. Frida's mother, Doña Matilde, was upset that her daughter was marrying an atheist and "fat communist." Frida's father, Guillermo, more practical and cool-headed, met the news with equanimity. According to Frida, when Diego broke the news to him, he replied, "Notice that my daughter is a sick person and all her life she will be sick; she is intelligent, but not pretty. Think it over if you want, and if you wish to get married, I give you my permission." At the wedding itself, which was performed at Coyoacán's town hall by the mayor—a pulque dealer—a bemused Guillermo is supposed to have said, "Gentlemen, is it not true that we are play-acting?"[5]

The wedding party that began in the afternoon and stretched into the evening was a raucous affair and marked the beginning of a pattern that would last throughout the marriage. Lupe Marín, Rivera's ex-wife briefly showed up, insulted the new bride by lifting her skirt, and commenting, "You see these two sticks. These are the legs Diego now has instead of mine." Later, according to Frida, "Diego went on a drunken binge. . . . [H]e took out his pistol, he broke a man's little finger, and broke other things. Then we had a fight, and I left crying and went home. A few days passed and Diego came to fetch me and took me to [our new home]."[6]

Casting her lot with Diego, Frida resigned her membership in the Communist party, an act that must have been as painful for her as it was for Rivera. Neither she nor Rivera would ever renounce communism or what they saw as the goals of the Communist movement, broadly conceived. But for nineteen years, until she was readmitted to the Party in 1948 after undergoing the humiliating and Stalinist "self-criticism," she was banished from Party proceedings and often viewed with hostility and contempt by Party members.

But in 1929, this banishment was not the most important event in Frida's life. In spite of the obvious problems and contradictions of living with a man like Diego Rivera, theirs was a relationship, a chemistry, that is still opaque to an outside observer. The other side of Rivera's obnoxious self-absorption, his constant self-mythologizing, and blatant tinkering with truth was a childlike playfulness and openness to those he loved. Clearly, Frida connected with him profoundly on this level. Equally clearly, she had found that he filled a need in her life. From the beginning she was proud of him, proud that he was her husband, yet this didn't mean she was a passive victim of his moods. As always, she was high-spirited and capable of holding her own. Nonetheless, at the beginning at least, she deferred to him and tried to figure out ways to please him and be his adoring *compañera*.

They soon became more than two people in a relationship. Somehow they melded into an organism greater than each of their individual selves. Losing a political party, Frida had thrown in her lot with another party, a party of two, Frida and Diego. They would become a pair that some of their friends would come to call, with as much irony as affection, "sacred monsters."

5

Colossus of the North

They thought I was a surrealist, but I wasn't.
I never painted dreams. I painted my life.

—*Frida Kahlo*

BY MARRYING DIEGO RIVERA, Frida had intentionally turned her life upside down. She was living in a new house near downtown Mexico City with an unpredictable husband, who maintained an almost superhuman work schedule, and who often stayed out all night with friends and visitors. Many of her friends in the Communist party now shunned her (on hearing the news of Rivera and Frida's wedding, Tine Modotti had archly commented, "Let's see how it turns out"), and she was trying to come to terms with her role in the marriage.

Fortunately for her and Rivera, they were about to benefit from a much-needed change of scene. In October, they were invited to a dinner at the residence of Mr. and Mrs. Dwight Morrow. Morrow, a well-connected New York lawyer and Republican party fat cat who had worked for the J. P. Morgan investment house and was a partner in the recently organized Kennecott Mining Company, was the Hoover administration's ambassador to Mexico. However, unlike past U.S ambassadors, Morrow wasn't an oligarchical troglodyte. A cultured man, Morrow saw himself as an emissary of enlightened capitalism.

Frida and Diego at an opening, New York, 1933.

Morrow proposed to Rivera that he begin work on a series of murals at the Cortés Palace in Cuernavaca, a magnificent colonial structure built in 1530 by the Spanish conquistador Hernán Cortés. Once Cortés's home and administrative headquarters, the palace now belonged to the state of Morelos. Morrow said that the U.S. government would pay Rivera twelve thousand dollars—a small fortune in Mexico in those days—to paint a fresco showing the history of the state of Morelos on the walls of the palace's loggia. It would be a gift from the people of the United States to the people of Mexico. And, Morrow said, because he and his wife would be away at a naval conference in London for much of 1930, the Riveras could stay in their residence in Cuernavaca while they worked on the murals.

Even though he had already made a commitment for the huge mural project at the National Palace, Rivera accepted Morrow's offer at once. He wanted to take a break from the Communist infighting in the capital, and the pay for the work in Cuernavaca was much better than that commissioned by the Mexican government. By December Frida and Diego had moved to Cuernavaca, a small and very beautiful city about ninety-minutes' drive from the capital.

In Mexico City and now in Cuernavaca Frida set about devising ways to endear herself to her husband. She learned from Lupe Marín what Rivera's favorite foods were (Marín and Frida had quickly made up after the disastrous wedding party). As Lupe Marín had done, Frida began showing up at the scaffolds in Cuernavaca with baskets of food at lunch, and often stayed at the site into the afternoon and evening helping Diego with her comments and suggestions of his drawings and with other tasks around the site. Diego valued Frida's quick and unconventional mind and he especially valued her sharp and unpretentious criticisms. As the years progressed he would come to increasingly depend on her judgments.

Perhaps the greatest adaptation Frida made in habits to please her husband was the sudden and dramatic change in her attire. Prior to 1930, she had tried on different personas that were expressed through different modes of dress. During her years at the Preparatoria, she had transformed herself from smart but obedient schoolgirl (wearing her German-gymnasium-influenced skirt and straw hat) to smart but defiant bohemian (when she took to wearing well-tailored men's suits with a short haircut—this before Chanel had made this a fashionable look in Europe). After her conversion to Communist orthodoxy, she briefly sported a working-class militant look: overalls, or a denim shirt and red tie with simple wool or denim dress and no ornamentation or jewelry other than a Communist red star on her collar or shirt pocket. But Rivera liked the dress of the women from the Tehuantepec Peninsula of Mexico. By taking the Tehuana dress Frida was further adopting Mexicanism. She began appearing in the clothes that would become her trademark: brightly colored and embroidered Tehuantepec blouses, full skirts, often complicated hair arrangements with ribbons, and lots of jewelry, sometimes heavy pre-Colombian pieces, other times colonial gold filigree, or mixtures of both or other different elements.

It would be an understatement to say that this Tehuana dress was not a style favored by most Mexican women (unless they were Tehuantepec Indians). By choosing to dress as she did, she at once pleased Rivera and made herself stand out vividly from others. Also the full blouses and long skirts hid the leg braces and torso corsets that she often had to wear.

This style was in tune with Rivera's peculiar brand of left-wing Mexican nationalism. It was "primitive," thus in Rivera's eyes, more "authentic" than the regular street wear of most Mexican urbanites (this was also the view of American expatriates such as Carleton Beals). "The classic Mexican dress," Rivera commented, "has been created by people for people. The Mexican women who do not wear it do not belong to the people, but are mentally and emotionally dependent on a foreign class to which they belong, i.e., the great American and French bureaucracy."[1] Typically for Diego, this cockeyed theory of dress did not extend to him. He often wore clothes that made him look like a western sheriff or rancher, or in his cheap business suits like a receiving clerk at a Ford factory, not in the least bit influenced by "authentic" Indian dress.

All of Frida's attempts at being an ideal helpmeet and exemplar of revolutionary Mexican womanhood did not stop her husband from taking other lovers. Sometime during their stay in Cuernavaca, Rivera began (or perhaps continued) a liaison with one of his young American assistants, Ione Robinson. His trysts with Robinson and other short-lasting infidelities with some of his Indian models occurred on his periodic trips back to Mexico City to continue work on the National Palace murals.

Frida tried to shrug off these dalliances, saying later in her life "being the wife of Diego is the most marvelous thing in the world. . . . I let him play matrimony with other women. Diego is not anybody's husband and never will be. But he is a great *camarada*." This resigned statement, laden with hollow bravado, came from a woman who had long since made her accommodations with her husband. It doesn't seem to reflect the Frida of 1929 and 1930, a young woman of twenty-two and twenty-three who had not yet become so world-weary and who was doing everything she could to please Diego Rivera. Perhaps, too, she believed that she was the one special person who would hold his eye forever.

Preoccupied with Diego's whims, and experimenting with new identities through costume, Frida didn't leave herself a lot of time for her own art in Cuernavaca. She managed to paint a nude of an

Indian woman and a self-portrait. But the most striking art she made, one that was a precursor to the intensely personal style she would shortly develop, was a drawing of herself in which Diego was imagined as a fetus inside her womb. The drawing referred to the baby she had aborted after three months of pregnancy during their stay in Cuernavaca. The abortion occurred after a doctor had told Frida that the baby was in the wrong position and that it would be difficult for her ever to bear a child because of the injuries she had suffered in the tram wreck in 1925.

Frida did have the option of a cesarean delivery, but decided against it. This would be the first of five abortions and miscarriages she would endure, all of which caused her intense anguish. She may have believed that having children would be the ultimate way to possess her husband. At the least, children would have offered her a consolation for a marriage that fast was proving to be something other than the ecstatic union she had hoped for.

Frida was mistaken if she thought a child would bring her closer to Rivera. In fact, Rivera was repulsed by children. His negligence had contributed to the death of one of his children from pneumonia in Paris in October 1917. While that child, whom he had with his common-law wife, Angelica Beloff, became sicker in an unheated apartment, Rivera, according to Beloff, "[cavorted] with his friends in the cafés. He kept up this infantile routine even during the last three days and nights of our baby's life. Diego knew that I was keeping a constant vigil over the baby in a last desperate effort to save its life; still he didn't come home at all. When the child finally died Diego, naturally, was the one to have the nervous collapse."[2] Rivera also abandoned another child he had with a Parisian mistress and seldom saw the two children he had with Lupe Marín. Had Frida succeeded in having a child with Diego, she may have found that this was the one sure way for her relationship with him to end.

By the fall of 1930 the Riveras stay at Cuernavaca was drawing to a close. The Cortés Palace mural had been completed, and the Morrows were set to reoccupy their weekend house. But Rivera again had another project lined up, one that would take him to work for the first time in the heart of the capitalist beast. Ralph Stackpole, an artist who had known Diego during his Paris years, had persuaded the San Francisco Stock Exchange and the city's School of Fine Arts to let Rivera paint murals in their buildings.

The visit to San Francisco that began in November 1930 was Frida's first trip to the United States—a place that fascinated and frightened her. As in Cuernavaca, she generally maintained the pose of Diego's subordinate partner, although now and then there was a hint that her old independence and spunk had begun to reappear. The photographer Edward Weston, Tina Modotti's former lover, met Frida in San Francisco. "I photographed Diego again—his new wife—Frida—too," he wrote in his diary.

> She is in sharp contrast to Lupe [Rivera's former wife]—petite, a little doll alongside Diego, but a doll in size only, for she is strong and quite beautiful, shows very little of her father's German blood. Dressed in native costume even to huaraches [leather sandals], she causes much excitement in the streets of San Francisco. People stop in their tracks to look in wonder.[3]

Weston must have made Frida feel at ease. This was her first trip abroad; she loved San Francisco, but the habits and peculiarities of Americans annoyed her. On most occasions, she was quiet and seemed unsure of herself to her American acquaintances. "The city and bay are overwhelming," she wrote to a friend back in Mexico City. "[But] I don't particularly like the gringo people. They are all boring and they all have faces like unbaked rolls (especially the old women)." In fact, she seems to have made little effort to get to know people in San Francisco other than the American assistants who helped Diego on his murals.

Rivera, on the other hand, put himself in his usual nonstop campaign of work and play. One of the first orders of business was to choose a model for the San Francisco Stock Exchange mural. After a quick scouting of potential muses, he chose Helen Wills Moody, a champion tennis player, to represent the bounteous earth mother, California. In her hand she holds the riches of the land: pears, apples, grapes, wheat, oranges, while below an assemblage of workers, scientists, and technicians produce airplanes, mine gold, and perfect seed crops. As usual, Rivera had an affair with his model that extended for the course of the work on the mural. What was different this time was that Frida might have struck back, by instigating an affair with Cristina Hastings, the Italian wife of one of Rivera's assistants.

It is curious that at about the time Rivera was beginning his affair with Helen Moody (and later when he had an affair with sculptor Louise Nevelson in New York), Frida began complaining of a new physical ailment. For reasons unknown, her right foot began to turn out, which aggravated the tendons in the foot and ankle and made it difficult for her to walk. This condition— in all likelihood a psychosomatic response to Rivera's very public carrying on—prompted Frida to visit a local physician, Leo Eloesser, who was a friend of Rivera's.

Eloesser and Frida quickly became close friends and would remain so for the rest of her life. He was a hard-working and respected surgeon at San Francisco Hospital and a teacher at the Stanford Medical School. He could find no reason for her sudden foot problem, but did discover something that Frida's various other doctors had missed: Frida had scoliosis, a congenital deformation, usually a narrowing, of the spine that could cause nerve damage, and thus various sorts of leg problems. These sometimes worsened as the patient aged. This scoliosis might have been a contributing cause of her foot ailment, much more likely though it was stress. Furthermore, in Eloesser's opinion, stress, perhaps coupled with scoliosis, and not her accident, was the main cause of most of the back and leg problems that she had experienced throughout her life. A conservative physician, he did not recommend surgery, but counseled life-style changes, mainly a proper amount of rest and a good diet, advice that Frida routinely ignored.

Frida worked intently on her art in San Francisco. She produced several portraits of women as well as one of Leo Eloesser. She also painted a sort of wedding portrait of herself and Diego Rivera. In the wedding portrait, she borrows an element from Mexican colonial and folk art—the use of a legend held by a dove—which describes the place and circumstances of the painting (in this case that it was painted in San Francisco for Albert Bender, a wealthy San Franciscan who would become one of her patrons).

The most important painting that Frida worked on while in San Francisco was her portrait of plant breeder Luther Burbank, who had died a few years before Frida had arrived in San Francisco. Born back east, Burbank immigrated to Santa Rosa, California, just north of San Francisco, in 1873. There for fifty-three years he worked diligently developing plant and tree varieties that would be healthier and more productive than existing stock. In Frida's mind, Burbank and the incredible cornucopia of California's agricultural wealth that she had seen on her excursions out of the city went hand in hand. His was the guiding genius of California's apparently endless ability to produce an amazing variety of crops. To salute the spirit of this man, she fashioned her most original painting to date.

In *Luther Burbank* the horticulturalist occupies the center of the painting. His legs seem to fuse with a sawed-off tree

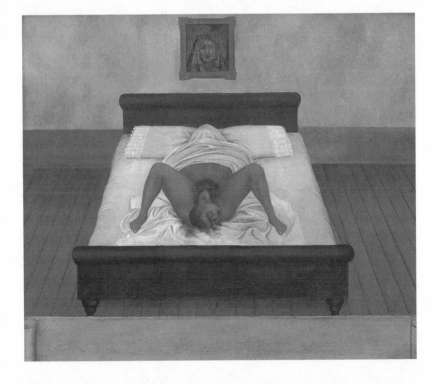

Opposite page top:
Henry Ford
Hospital, 1932.
Opposite page bottom:
My Birth, 1932.
Right: Luther
Burbank, 1931.
Below: Nineteenth-
century Mexican
ex-voto retablo for
Our Lady of
Lourdes.

trunk, which make him appear grafted to the trunk and its roots, which are visible in a cut-away view of the underlying earth. At the base of the roots, the viewer observes the plant fertilized by a buried body, perhaps Burbank's body, or his imagination or subconscious.

This is Frida's first clear fantasy painting, a work that explores something other than straight portraiture. *Luther Burbank*, although it is a portrait of a man, is also a dream vision of the subject's life. Through a contrast of the sere hills in the background and Burbank's flowering trees in the foreground, Frida celebrates the fruits of human imagination and drive. By contrasting the buried body that fertilizes the plant/man with the living creature aboveground, Frida begins to play with the duality of life/death, conscious/unconscious. In both cases, Frida seems to be saying, the latter fertilizes the former.

Frida may have been influenced by the Surrealist movement, which was in full flower in Europe at that time. She undoubtably was aware of the movement, although she may not yet have seen many examples of Surrealist paintings. But it is much more likely that *Luther Burbank* was a work that sprang directly from the imagination of Frida Kahlo, with only the smallest debt owed to European Surrealism.

Latin America in general and Mexico in particular, as several commentators have noted, is a place whose culture has nurtured a deep pool of organic Surrealism. "Pre-Columbian myths, Afro-American rites, the Baroque hunger for the object of desire, and the masks of religious syncretism," Carlos Fuentes has observed, "gave Latin America its own patent for Surrealism." Expressions of the duality of life and death are good example of this. Xipe Totec, the Aztec Lord of the Flayed Skin, possessed a dualistic nature that was surrealistic in the extreme.

The skin of his flayed victim, which Xipe Totec ritualistically wore, also refers to the snake-like shedding of his own skin and signifies renewal, even resurrection. Xipe Totec is at once the god of spring and renewal, and the god who inflicts syphilitic blisters and festering on his human devotees. Frida, who was steeped in Aztec and Maya mythology, was aware of Xipe Totec and the other ancient gods. Her Surrealism was home grown.[4]

But Frida's outlook was profoundly different from that of the Surrealists. Unlike the disillusioned European Surrealists, who were measuring the depths of their subconscious and dream world in search of an escape from the limits of reason—Frida was searching for a means of expressing and coming to terms with reality.

With their work completed in California, in June 1931, Diego and Frida briefly returned to Mexico City. With the money he had earned in Cuernavaca and California, Diego paid off the mortgage of the Blue House, the Kahlo family home in Coyoacán, and began building a connected house/studio for himself and Frida in nearby San Angel. The Mexican government was putting pressure on him to hurry up with his work at the National Palace, but Rivera had his mind elsewhere. In his own words, he had seen a country "hurrying to the future" and he wanted to be immersed in its drama.

Frida wrote her new friend Dr. Eloesser that summer from Mexico City:

> Diego is not happy here since he misses the friendliness of the people of San Francisco as well as the city itself, now he wants nothing other than to return to the United States to paint. . . . Mexico is as always disorganized and gone to the devil, the only thing that it retains is the immense beauty of the land and of the Indians. Each day the United States' ugli-

ness steals away a piece of it, it is a sad thing but people must eat and it can't be helped that the big fish eats the little one.

In November, Frida and Rivera traveled to New York for the first time. Rivera was being given a one-man show at the newly created Museum of Modern Art. This marked a huge success for Rivera, as it was only the second one-man show to have been presented at that institution (the other one had been for Matisse).

Again Frida was presented with the spectacle of advanced capitalism North American-style, and again she was of two minds about how to react to it. On one hand, she could not help but be dazzled by the dynamism of New York; its impressive new skyline dotted with sky-piercing buildings such as the Chrysler and Empire State buildings. On the other hand, by 1931 the Great Depression had begun to squeeze the life out of the less fortunate members of American society. "Here society turns me off," she wrote Dr. Eloesser in late November,

and I feel a bit of a rage against all these rich guys here, since I have seen thousands of people in the most terrible misery without anything to eat and with no place to sleep, that is what has most impressed me here, it is terrifying to see the rich having parties day and night while thousands and thousands of people are dying of hunger.

Although Frida's critique of American society was perfectly accurate, there is a strange absence at its core. Forgetting New York's glitz, which etched a sharper contrast between rich and poor, almost exactly the same thing could have been said about the conditions of poverty and the relations between rich and poor in Mexico City. It is as if Frida were unaware of the conditions on the city's east side, where recently arrived immigrants from the countryside still huddled together in shanty-towns in conditions even worse than Depression-era New York. In fact, she may not have known firsthand of the depth and extent of poverty in her own country. Despite the veneer of Marxism she wore like body armor, she was in many ways politically naïve; an upper-middle-class woman who lived at a distance from many of the harsh realities of her country. In Mexico she was a creature of a fairly unvarying routine. She painted, went to parties and protest rallies with Diego, but her life does not seem to have actually taken her into urban slums or poor rural hamlets. In America she seems to have seen the ugly face of poverty for the first time.

The show at the Museum of Modern Art—which drew critical acclaim and the largest attendance of any exhibit at the museum to that date—set Rivera on a roll in the United States. In the spring of 1932, he and Frida went to Detroit where he had been commissioned to complete a large mural in the lobby of the Detroit Institute of Arts. Rivera was euphoric about the Detroit commission. One thing that drew him to Detroit was his love of machines as objects, as works of art, in themselves. He described the machinery and factories as "being as beautiful as the early Mayan and Aztec sculptures. . . . I now placed the collective hero, man-and-machine, higher than the old traditional heroes of art and legend." Also, for Diego Rivera, Detroit epitomized twentieth-century American capitalism. Here was the heart of industrial America. Here were its most advanced machines, its princes of capitalism—and its proletariat. A firm believer in Marx, Rivera thought that revolution would only occur in those places where capitalism was most advanced. That place was Detroit.

Frida was less enthralled. Detroit, she wrote to Dr. Eloesser, "seems like a shabby old village. I don't like it at all, but I am happy because Diego is working very happily here, and he has found a lot of material for his frescoes that he will do in the museum. He is enchanted with the factories, the machines, etc. like a child with a new toy."

Frida and Rivera again plunged into the high society of an American city, this time in the unlikely company of Henry and Edsel Ford. Perhaps feeling more comfortable at last in the United States, Frida's outrageous personality begins to show itself. Knowing that Henry Ford was a famous anti-Semite, she asked him at a dinner party, "Mr. Ford, are you Jewish?" The jibe must have rolled off the old industrialist's back; later at another get-together, he admired her Tehuantepec clothes and repeatedly asked her to dance.

Frida had barely arrived in Detroit when she discovered that she was again pregnant. Given the warnings that had been issued to her by doctors in the past, the news of her pregnancy caused her great concern. She still wanted a child, yet she also was fearful that the delivery of a child might kill her. In May she wrote a fretful letter to the one doctor she could trust, Leo Eloesser. Her doctor in Detroit had said that he saw no reason why she could not have a baby; it could be delivered by cesarean section. "Naturally, I am willing to do what you think is best for my health," she told Eloesser.

> Do you think it would be more dangerous to abort than to have a child? . . . You better than anyone know what condition I am in. In the first place with this heredity in my blood [she is referring to her father's epilepsy] I do not think that the child could come out very healthy. In the second place, I am not strong and the pregnancy will weaken me more. . . . Here [in Detroit] I have no one in my family who could take care of me during and after the pregnancy, since poor Diego, no matter how much he wants to take care of me,

cannot, since he has in addition the problem of work and thousands of things. . . . Diego is as always good to me but I do not want to distract him with such things now that he is burdened with all the work and more than anything needs tranquillity and calm.[5]

Before she received a reply from Eloesser, Frida made up her mind. This time she would have the child. Her Detroit doctor ordered her to rest, but she ignored him and continued going out to help Diego at the mural site and took up driving lessons. Early in the morning of July 4, Frida began hemorrhaging and was taken to Detroit's Henry Ford Hospital. For most of the day she bled huge clots of blood out of her womb.

Convinced that it was a sign that she would never have a child, Frida was seized by despair. According to a friend, she cried out, "I wish I were dead! I don't know why I have to go on living like this." Gradually, however, through her grief she began to accept the miscarriage. "There is nothing to do but put up with it," she wrote a friend, "I have a cat's luck." And she found a way to sort through her pain by painting one of her most profound works, *Henry Ford Hospital.*

Painted later in the month of July 1932, *Henry Ford Hospital* marked a dramatic breakthrough in Frida's art. Bleeding and lying naked on a bed that is surreally floating and slightly tilted up and toward the viewer, Frida occupies the center of the painting. In the background is the Ford Motor Company's Rouge plant. Floating in the nether space she occupies, but surrounding her bed, are six objects that are attached to her by red veins/ribbons. Above her are the fetus of her baby, a snail, and a stylized drawing of a woman's torso mounted on a pedestal; below is a mechanical device that looks somewhat like a lock, a purple orchid, and a drawing of the pelvic bones, the shattered structure that Frida believed was the cause of her miscarriage.

All of the objects had immediate significance in Frida's life. The snail was her way of conceptualizing the agonizing slowness of her miscarriage. The drawing of the woman's torso shows her damaged spine and sperm wending its way to the uterus. The mechanical lock could be an instrument of torture, or a symbol of the denial of motherhood. And the orchid was a copy of the flower that Rivera had given her while she lay in recovery. "When I painted it," she said of the orchid, "I had an idea of a sexual thing mixed with the sentimental."

What marks this painting with greatness is the completely unsentimental and breathtaking originality with which Frida investigates this moment in her life. Her body is not portrayed as an object of desire or in a flattering way; her stomach is distended by pregnancy and a tear comes from her eyes. A viewer can see the truth to the remark she made later that she—unlike the European Surrealists—painted her life, not her dreams.

Yet, even though the power of this painting lies in the shocking clarity in which her miscarriage is portrayed, its enchantment rests in the symbols Frida has invented to narrate this event and the way she had rendered them so that they seem as much like a dream as an objective fact. It is the mix of brutal clarity and dreamlike symbolism that gives this work a spiritual power. The painting shines a light into Frida's soul like no letter she wrote or remark she made ever could. *Henry Ford Hospital* and the works that followed are the essence of her spiritual path. They show her successfully grappling in the language she knew best—her visual vocabulary—with the universal problems of pain, suffering, and death. Later, Rivera noting the change her art took with this painting said, "Frida began on a series of masterpieces which had no precedent in the history of art—paintings which exalted the feminine qualities of endurance of truth, reality, cruelty, and suffering. Never before had a woman put such agonized poetry on canvas as Frida did at this time in Detroit."

With only one interruption, Frida would remain in Detroit until March 1933. In September she was called back to Mexico by the illness of her mother, who had been diagnosed as having breast cancer. Even though Frida was saddened by her mother's suffering, and eventual death on September 15, she was overjoyed to be back in Mexico. For her Mexico represented a preindustrial world, a traditional world where people still made their living from the land. This romantic and sentimental view, of course, didn't square with Frida's self-professed Marxism, but she never was a rigorous political thinker. Mexico was her home, the place she felt most comfortable. She longed to remain there and not have to return to the United States. The United States she saw was a barren industrial wasteland and the place where she had lost a baby and might yet lose a husband.

While Frida was in Mexico she wrote a letter to Diego that shows the complexity of her feeling for him. After an abortion and a miscarriage, Frida's need for a deep and absolute connection with another person had grown even as its nature had changed. In place of the need for the approval of a great man, she now began to substitute the unconditional love of a mother for a son, specifically an infant son.

> Although you tell me that you see yourself as very ugly, . . . I don't believe it, I know how handsome you are anyway and the only thing I regret is not to be there to kiss you and take care of you and even if I would sometimes bother you with my grumbling. I adore you my Diego. I feel as though I left my child with no one and that you need me . . . I cannot live

without my chiquito lindo [my handsome little one]. The house without you is nothing. Everything without you seems horrible to me.[6]

In October she returned to her three-hundred-pound baby, only to find that in her absence he had gone on a wacky orange, grapefruit, and vegetable juice diet. In the words of one of Rivera's biographers, he looked like a "half-inflated barrage balloon." Frida set about at once to cook for him and reinflate him to his normal weight.

Returning to her art with the memory of her mother's death and her miscarriage still fresh in her mind, Frida painted another riveting work, which she titled *My Birth*. In it the viewer is again faced with an uncompromising scene of suffering and tragedy. The head and neck of what appears to be a dead baby with joined eyebrows (Frida imagining herself as a baby) dangles from the womb of a dead mother, whose face is covered with a sheet. Above the birth/death bed, an image of the Virgin Mary, the Virgin of Sorrows, pierced by daggers, grieves over the scene. Frida said of the painting, "My head is covered, because, coincidentally, with the painting of the picture, my mother died." Thus Frida indicates that she is not only the child being born in the painting, but the mother giving birth as well.

My Birth was the first of a series of paintings in which Frida intended to illustrate every year of her life. The Virgin of Sorrows shown over the bed in the painting was an actual image that her religious mother had in their house, and the room depicted in the painting was the room of the Casa Azul in which Frida was born. This painting is extraordinary because it is at once a memorial to Frida's recently deceased mother, a revisiting of the miscarriage that was still so fresh in her memory, and an expression of the moment she came into the world. In *My Birth*, Frida is staking out an imaginative terrain that is intensely personal, yet not leadenly factual. It is a painting of the interior world of feeling fused with the exterior world of biography, and it is a painting that could only have been imagined by a woman. This particular bleak image of suffering and loss in childbirth was absolutely new in the history of art.

Both *My Birth* and *Henry Ford Hospital* were executed on tin, the medium favored by Mexican folk painters of devotional works called *retablos. Retablos* often feature ex-voto pleas by the sufferer or members of his or her family asking Christ or the Virgin Mary for cures. The borrowing of this material and style was an intriguing and appropriate choice for Frida to make. The blank legend at the bottom of *My Birth*, suggests that no plea or even identification of this work was necessary. However, in later paintings, Frida often inserted text that explained or commented on the visual images.

Rivera had suggested that painting on tin might work well with what Frida wanted to do, and she had immediately understood that he was right. It also probably was at this time that Frida began to collect these nineteenth- and twentieth-century art works—a large group of which hang in the Casa Azul—now the Frida Kahlo Museum.

In March 1933, Frida and Diego were invited to come back to New York where Rivera had been commissioned to paint what might have been the most important mural of his life—a fresco in the lobby of the newly built RCA Building in Rockefeller Center—epicenter of American capitalism. However, from the beginning this project began to sour. Rivera gave the mural the unwieldy title, *Men at the Crossroads Looking with Hope and High Vision to the Choosing of a New and Better Future*. Before Rivera was able to finish the work, he was attacked by the conservative *New York World-Telegram*. "Rivera Paints Scenes of Communist Activity and John D. Jr. Foots Bill," the *World-Telegram* headline screamed.

Rivera believed that the decisions made about Rockefeller Center came from his patrons, notably John D. Rockefeller, Jr. and John D. Jr.'s brother, Nelson. In fact, management of the complex fell to the Todd Corporation, who, unlike the Rockefellers had little interest in art and its complexities. When the Todds found out that Rivera had prankishly substituted the head of Lenin for what was supposed to be a generic labor leader, they decided they didn't need the publicity that the project was garnering. Suddenly on May 9, 1933, he was handed a check for the balance of his fee, fourteen thousand dollars, and escorted out of the building. The Todds waited until the following February to demolish the work.

The Rockefeller Center fiasco marked the end of Diego's public art career in the United States. His high hopes of becoming the working man's spokesman in the center of world capitalism has suddenly evaporated, as had any chance of living and working in the United States. As if to remind him of the fractious atmosphere he had hoped to leave behind forever, a Mexico City newspaper, *Excelsior*, exulted in his failure: "Rivera is a painter of ugliness . . . nature did not grace him with white skin and blue eyes so he avenges himself by painting ugly types."

Still Rivera insisted on lingering in Manhattan, hoping something would come up. As days became weeks, he and Frida argued about returning to Mexico. She had been ready to go back for months. He said he never wanted to return. One day, during yet another argument about their plans, Diego pulled a knife and slashed a painting he had been working on. It was a study of desert cacti that he had transformed into outstretched hands. "I don't want to go back to that!" he screamed.

Finally in December, Rivera was forced to admit defeat. On

December 20, they took a steamer back to Mexico. Frida was ecstatic. Her painful, yet artistically fruitful stay in "Gringolandia" was over. She was coming home to live and work. There was no reason to believe that she and Diego could not make a new beginning of their life and art together.

Frida in her studio at the Blue House, ca. 1943.

6

La Chingada

Who is the *Chingada?* Above all, she is the Mother. Not a
Mother of flesh and blood, but a mythical figure.

—*Octavio Paz*

DIEGO RIVERA RETURNED TO MEXICO a frustrated and resent-
ful man, his dream of becoming an art star in the United
States shattered. For the first few months of 1934 he lay
around his new house and studio in San Angel in a stupor.
Emotionally and physically spent, he had to be hospitalized
several times for kidney problems and various other ailments
imagined and real.

Physically Frida wasn't faring well either. She had to have
her appendix removed, and soon after she arrived home, she
found out she was pregnant again. This time, not wanting to risk
another miscarriage, she had an abortion.

The place they had come to, the apartment/studio combination in the southern Mexico City suburb of San Angel, had only
recently been completed. Rivera had designed two Bauhaus
International structures to be built side by side on a single lot.
On one side, Rivera had his own spacious studio and living quar-
ters; next to Rivera's building was Frida's smaller house and studio. The two buildings were linked by a walkway that went from
one roof to the other. Unintentionally, they neatly symbolized

Frida and Diego's relationship from Rivera's point of view: together but detached, separate but unequal, outwardly untraditional but inwardly cleaving to the ancient codes of *machismo*.

As Rivera recovered his strength, he began searching for someone to blame for his New York fiasco. The Mexican people were a convenient target, although as a professed Marxist it would be unseemly to blame the very group he supposedly was giving his artistic vision to defend. So he kept this complaint private, mainly vented in outbursts to Frida. In a letter to Dr. Eloesser, Frida transmitted Diego's tirades:

> In relation to Diego's work, the people here [in Mexico] always respond with obscenities and dirty tricks, and this is what makes him most desperate since he has only to arrive and they start attacking him in the newspapers. . . . Here he does no more than finish a fresco and the next week it is already scratched and spat on with phlegm.[1]

But the person who absorbed most of the blame for Rivera's unwanted return to Mexico was Frida Kahlo herself.

As soon as he felt better, Diego holed up in his part of the studio and began drawing, mainly nudes. One of the first nudes he sketched sometime in the late spring or early summer was of Frida's younger sister, Cristina. Cristina had been separated from her husband since 1930 and was living with her two children at the Casa Azul. Either that spring or in the summer, the two of them began an affair.

Frida does not seem to have discovered her husband's latest escapade until mid to late summer 1934. When she did, she was devastated. She viewed this latest sexual engagement as something far beyond the ordinary Riveraesque fling. The affair with Cristina was a serious breach of trust and an attack—retribution—against Frida for their return to Mexico. She wrote a friend that she felt like she had been "murdered by life." Again—as it almost always seemed to do when Rivera was flaunting an affair—her damaged right foot, the part of her body that acted as the receptacle of pain and tension, began to cause her trouble. Probably against Dr. Eloesser's advice (Frida was writing him regularly now about her personal and medical problems), she elected to have surgery on her foot in the fall. This would be the beginning of many surgeries (perhaps as many as twenty), most of them in Leo Eloesser's opinion unnecessary, that she would have until her death in 1954.

Because he was a transparent and predictable creature, it isn't a leap to understand why Rivera had the affair with Cristina. Rivera's emotional development had reached and stopped at the level of a boy—and an extremely narcissistic boy at that. This particular affair was his way of punishing someone for his own failures and what more convenient person to punish than the person nearest at hand. The need to punish was not an unconscious impulse, but a deliberate one. In his autobiography he wrote, "If I loved a woman, the more I loved her, the more I wanted to hurt her. Frida was only the most obvious victim of this disgusting trait."

There is one writer whose thoughts about cruelty and betrayal in the Mexican context help make sense of what Rivera did, and how Frida eventually came to grips with her anguish (though her wounds would never heal). Octavio Paz has written penetratingly about the intertwining themes of culture and the relations between the sexes in his country. At the crux of this relationship is the verb *chingar* (literally "to screw," but more precisely to "hurt," "wound," or in the most extreme cases "to kill"). The one who acts on this impulse is usually, but not always, a man. The one on the receiving end, the *chingada*, is most frequently a woman. The reason typically given for this act of psychic or physical violence is betrayal.

According to Paz, the dynamic—the need for a man to hurt a woman—originates at the very beginning of modern Mexican history, that is, at the time of the Spanish conquest. The first betrayal was by the Indian woman known as La Malinche. She became Cortes's lover and acted as his translator and advisor during his audacious and triumphant march of conquest. Thus, she betrayed in the most profound sense the Indians' nations of Mexico. On a less cosmic level, the act of conquest itself was so brutal and long-lasting that it set a pattern in Mexican society. The more powerful could always *chingar* the weak. The weak in turn could extract some measure of revenge by a betrayal, which in turn engendered another act of retribution by the powerful. As Paz explains, "In Mexico there are only two possibilities in life: either he inflicts the actions implied by *chingar* on others, or else he suffers them himself at the hands of others." According to Paz:

> All our anxious tensions express themselves in a [single] phrase we use when anger, joy or enthusiasm cause us to exalt our conditions as Mexican. . . . ¡Viva Mexico, hijos de la chingada! [Long live Mexico, children of the violated woman].

Diego had made Frida his *chingada*. He wanted to hurt and wound her for the perceived hurt and wound he imagined she had inflicted on him. This need to wound is seen even more clearly when Frida and Diego's relationship is understood as one of mother and son. Beginning even before they went to the United States, Frida was referring to Rivera as her baby, her child. According to Paz, in Mexico there is no act of wounding more potent and satisfying that the symbolic wounding of mother by son. Paz concludes:

> The Mexican conceives of love as combat and conquest. . . . It is not so much an attempt to penetrate reality by means of the body as it is to violate it. . . . In a sense, all of us, by the simple fact of being born of woman, are hijos de la Chingada, sons of Eve.

What is not so easy to understand is why Cristina Kahlo entered into the affair with Rivera. The two sisters were only a year apart in age, but were vastly different in temperament. Physically, Frida was thin and angular, Cristina plump and Rubenesque. Frida was vibrant and magnetic and thrust herself into the world, especially in Mexico City where she felt most comfortable. Cristina was quite her opposite. Where Frida was wildly imaginative, Cristina was prosaic. "She lives a little bit in the ether," Frida said condescendingly of her sister. "If she goes to a movie she always asks, well, but who is the informer? who is the assassin? who is the girl?, in sum, she does not understand either the beginning or the end, and in the middle [she falls asleep]."[2] Perhaps, at least on some level, Cristina wanted to hurt an older sister she saw as overbearing and patronizing.

The affair stunned Frida. Trying to sort through these feelings, she wrote to Bertram and Ella Wolfe, "I had trusted Diego would change, but I can see and know that it is impossible. It's just a whim on my part. Naturally, I should have understood from the beginning that it will not be me who will make him live in this way or that way, especially when it comes to such a matter."[3] Later in the same letter she assesses her value in relation to Rivera:

> First, he has his work, which protects him from many things,

and then his adventures, which keep him entertained. People look for him and not me. I know that, as always, he is full of concerns and worries for his work; however, he lives a full life without the emptiness of mine. I have nothing because I don't have him. I never thought he was everything to me and that, separated from him, I was like a piece of trash. I thought I was helping him to live as much as I could, and that I could solve any situation in my life alone without complications of any kind. But now I realize that I don't have any more than any other girl disappointed at being dumped by her man. I am worth nothing, I know how to do nothing; I cannot be on my own.

My situation seems so ridiculous and stupid to me that you can't imagine how I dislike and hate myself. I've lost my best years being supported by a man, doing nothing else but what I thought would benefit and help him. I never thought about myself, and after six years, his answer is that fidelity is a bourgeois virtue and that it exists only to exploit and to obtain economic gain.[4]

One of the first things Frida did after recovering from her shock of betrayal and depression was cut her hair short and drop her Tehuana clothes. For a while (until she forgave Rivera and Cristina) she dressed in more or less standard women's clothes of the period and no longer donned her jewelry.

She made no art in 1934 and only two works in 1935. However, one of the two 1935 paintings must rank as a masterpiece, again another brilliant transmutation of personal anguish into a powerful work of art. The painting is called *A Few Small Nips*. At the center of the painting is a murdered woman lying on a bloodied bed, her arm outstretched in the manner of a sculpture or painting showing the dead Christ after he has been removed from the cross. The woman is naked except for a shoe, sock, and garter on one leg, the garter suggesting that the woman may have been a prostitute. Her murderer, presumably her aggrieved lover, stands over her, with a grim smile of satisfaction on his lips. Blotches of blood red paint even smear the picture frame, indicating that the horror of the crime cannot be contained in the painting. Ironic doves, the messengers of peace, carry a banner at the top of the painting: *Unos Cuantos Piquetitos*—"a few small nips." The slogan came from an article Frida had seen in a Mexico City newspaper about the murder of a woman by her husband. "But I only gave her a few small nips," the man had been quoted as saying. This black sort of humor, which gives the work a strange and potent mixture of horror and humor—and which laughs at death—is distinctly Mexican in character.

As in *Henry Ford Hospital* and *My Birth*, Frida had painted this small work on tin, the medium of the *retablos*. This time though she had borrowed the theme and to some degree the composition from the Mexican artist she greatly admired, José Guadalupe Posada. In 1890, Posada had illustrated a story about a famous Mexican rapist-murderer named Francisco Guerrero with a lithograph of a man slitting a woman's throat. Frida, who kept collections of Posada's work at her house, probably had seen this particular illustration, of if she hadn't she certainly was familiar with many other examples of his style. Like Frida Kahlo, Posada reveled in the gritty details of Mexican street life. But unlike Frida, he never sought to fuse these scenes with a personal mythology to create transcendent art.

By painting *A Few Small Nips* Frida was again able to give voice through her visual language to something that had happened to her directly, this time Rivera's wounding infidelity with her sister. Brilliantly she has fused this personal and brutal anguish with something larger—the national myth of *La Chingada*—the

A Few Small Nips, 1935.

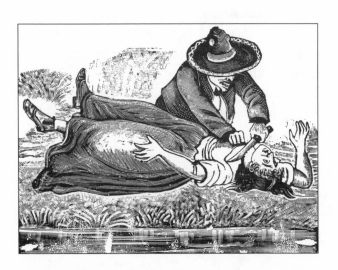

José Guadalupe Posada, Victim of Francisco Guerrero, 1890.

woman killed or wounded because of a perceived betrayal.

Through *A Few Small Nips*, Frida seems to have exorcised the pain, even bitterness that was inside her, or at least enough to enable her to make decisions about what to do next. By the summer of 1935 she had moved out of the Bauhaus bungalow that she had shared with Rivera and into an apartment near the center of the city. She continued to see Diego regularly, usually several times a week at least, visiting him at the studio in San Angel or meeting him for parties or performances in the city. She was attempting to position herself semi-independently of him while also admitting her need for him. This was a psychologically dangerous balancing act, for by baldly admitting her need for him she was making herself vulnerable to continuing emotional manipulation via the threat of abandonment.

Having in her own mind come to a sort of a cease-fire with her husband, Frida traveled in July 1935 with two women friends to New York for a much-needed respite from Diego Rivera and everything he stood for. Bravely (and perhaps, masochistically) she explains herself in a letter to Rivera written in New York:

> [I know now that] the letters, the problems with the skirts, the female teachers of . . . "English," the Gypsy models, helpers with "good will," "plenipotentiary women sent from faraway places," are just simply jokes, and that deep inside you and I love each a lot. Even if we experience endless adventures, beatings on doors, "mentions" of our mothers, and international complaints, don't we always love each other? I think that what is happening is that I am a little stupid and a fool because all these things have happened and have repeated themselves during the seven years that we have lived together. All the anger has simply made me understand better that I love you more than my own skin,

and that, even though you don't love me as much, you love me a little anyway.

She ended her letter with a heartbreaking query: "Don't you? If this is not true, I'll always be hopeful that it should be, and that's enough for me."[5]

Back in Mexico City by late summer, Frida put her shaky, new independence to a provisional test by beginning affairs with two men, the Mexican muralist Ignacio Aguirre and American sculptor Isamu Noguchi. Even though Frida now saw herself as free to live her life as she pleased with whomever she pleased, she was careful to keep these two particular relations, and all subsequent relations with men, hidden from her nominal husband, Diego Rivera.

Diego freely admitted that he didn't mind Frida carrying on lesbian affairs, but that her affairs with other men drove him insanely jealous. He also told her that he would rectify any such lapses on her part with a pistol. Apparently, even though in general his machismo was more bluster than real, more theater than actual physical violence, Rivera made good on his threat of at least demonstrating violent intent sometime in the fall of 1935 when he somehow discovered Frida's liaison with Noguchi.

According to Noguchi, Rivera came to the Blue House, where the two lovers clandestinely met, "with a gun. He always carried a gun." Noguchi then had to hurriedly gather his clothes and scramble over the courtyard wall to get away before Rivera came storming in, a scene at once comic and sinister. Noguchi added, "The second time he displayed his gun to me was in the hospital. Frida was ill for some reason, and I went there, and he showed me his gun, and said, "Next time I see you, I'm going to shoot you."

This laughable exaggerated phallic posturing seems to have cooled Noguchi's passion, and it also complicates and darkens any portrait we might try to paint of Frida Kahlo. Why did she put up with this nonsense? What, if anything, had she gained by her charade of a semi-independent existence from her husband? Clearly her affairs with men, which seem to have begun in earnest in this period, had about them an element of convoluted role-playing. Frida Kahlo, the Marxist bohemian who scorned bourgeois respectability, converts to Frida Kahlo, naughty housewife who wants, even thrills, in being "caught" in an "infidelity" by a man who is incapable of understanding the meaning of that word. It was as if she wanted to play Russian roulette with herself and her lovers so that she could incite Rivera's jealousy and remind him that she was worthy of being possessed.

Frida seems to have been unable to figure a way out of the trap of *La Chingada*, the cruel cycle of aggression and betrayal visited on women who remain in relationships with men like Diego Rivera. Instead she established a framework within which she would try to lessen the sting of her insurmountable dependency on her estranged husband. Understood in this light, Frida's new sexual "independence" was neither completely independent nor conducted on her own terms. Her conduct and behavior from this point on was still based on a motivation that remained unchanged since the beginning of her marriage: what she wanted more than anything, what she openly admitted in her letter of July 1935, was to gain and hold the undivided attention and loyalty of her husband, a losing battle as she admitted, but one she would never give up.

By 1936, having constructed a new calculus for her relationship with Diego, Frida forgave her sister Cristina and dismissed the Diego-Cristina affair with her legendary (and often masked) alegría. Wounds apparently healed, she began visiting Cristina's house often to see her sister and her two children, Isolde and

Antonio. Before long, the children began staying with her when she eventually moved back into her side of the bungalow at Rivera's compound in San Angel. The children became her surrogates for the children that she now realized she'd never have.

Even though Frida was back in San Angel, she had not returned to the same arrangement with Diego that had existed before the affair with Cristina. She now frequently locked her side of the complex so that Rivera could not come and go to see her at will. She also ventured out into the city much more often on her own. It was at about this time that she began frequenting working-class cantinas and dance halls, and drinking more. The girl who Lupe Marín said, "drank like a Mariachi" now began slowly to become addicted to alcohol. Frida never saw this as a major problem, and even joked about. "I drank because I wanted to drown my sorrows," she wrote a friend. "Now the damned thing has learned to swim."

Frida still made a point of being at San Angel with Rivera for the many informal gatherings occasioned by visiting artists and celebrities. The American writer John Dos Passos, Mexican photographer Manuel Alvarez Bravo, Mexican film stars such as Dolores Del Rio, even Mexican president Lázaro Cárdenas all made their way to the studio in San Angel to partake of the famous alegría of the Rivera-Kahlo household.

One of the most famous and ill-starred personalities of the 1930s landed, on the run, in 1937 on Mexican soil. Leon Trotsky had been a hunted man since he had lost a power struggle with Joseph Stalin for leadership of the Soviet Communist party following Lenin's death in 1924. By 1927 he had been expelled from the Party; in 1929 the Soviet government sent him into exile. Stalin soon realized that he had made a mistake in letting Trotsky leave the Soviet Union and ordered his secret police to kill him, an assignment that proved difficult and would take eleven years to achieve.

Trotsky spent the next eight years holed up with bodyguards in one decaying rural estate after another, first in Turkey, then in France and Norway. None of the leaders of these nations wanted to permanently host Trotsky, and he was always in danger of being sent to a new refuge as a result of Soviet government pressure on the countries in which he stayed. With the election of leftist Mexican president Lázaro Cárdenas in 1934, Trotsky's supporters thought they had found a sympathetic head of state, one who would grant him permanent refugee status. With Diego Rivera at the vanguard, negotiators reached an agreement with the Mexican government that allowed Trotsky to enter Mexico as a political refugee. He could write political manifestos and organize his supporters around the world, but he was to keep himself at a distance from Mexican politics.

Trotsky arrived on a rusty trawler in the Mexican port of Veracruz on January 9, 1937. Because Rivera had fallen ill, Frida was sent to greet him. Frida, Trotsky, his wife Natalia, and his entourage spent a night in Veracruz before proceeding by special train to Mexico City. Photos of his arrival show him dressed formally and surrounded by a swarm of uniformed and plainclothes police officers. At his side are Natalia and Frida. He was taken immediately to the Blue House in Coyoacán, which would be his home for the next two years. Guillermo Kahlo had to be moved into a daughter's house (Cristina was already established, probably by Rivera, in another nearby house) to make way for the fugitive-in-waiting.

Since his expulsion from the Communist party, Rivera had been looking for a home for himself somewhere in the non-Stalinist Communist left. The dispute between Stalin and Trotsky offered him a perfect place to land. He joined Trotsky's Fourth

International, a worldwide but anemic alternative to the Stalinist Communist party, and began attempting to annoy his old Communist comrades in Mexico by extolling the virtues of Trotsky and denouncing the evils of Stalin. Frida was not as interested in the minutiae of Communist dogmatic schisms as Rivera, but because he had sided with Trotsky, she followed suit, although she never officially joined the Trotskyite party in Mexico.

Frida and Rivera knew that it was dangerous to harbor Trotsky, but they reveled in frisson of harboring a world-famous fugitive. They expected virulent quarrels with the likes of their ex-friend David Alfaro Siquieros, a painter and, next to Rivera himself, one of the best-known muralists in Mexico. Siquieros was a rabid Stalinist and had remained active in the Mexican Communist party. Like Rivera, Siquieros habitually carried a revolver slung Wyatt Earp-style on a belt and holster around his waist. Unlike Rivera, Siquieros was a genuine gunman who had served as a soldier during the Mexican Revolution. Rivera knew not to provoke Siquieros too far.

Trotsky had been at the Casa Azul about six months when he and Frida began an affair. Like all of Frida's affairs with men, but even more so than usual, she kept this one secret. It was apparently short-lived, about a month or so, and Trotsky was much more the infatuated partner than she. She referred to him condescendingly as "the old man" and "Little Goatee." It must have been satisfying to her that her assignations with Trotsky were held at Cristina Kahlo's house with her sister's help. Frida had turned her betrayer into her confidante to strike back, for the moment in secret, against Rivera. On November 7, 1937, as if to memorialize and close out her affair with "the old man," Frida presented Trotsky with one of her self-portraits.

During this time the Republican and Nationalist armies were engaged in a civil war in Spain, a conflict that occupied Frida's energies more completely than intra-Communist intrigue in Mexico or faded Bolshevic leaders. She spent a good amount of time raising money in Mexico and abroad for the Republican cause.

When Frida left Mexico for a trip to New York and Paris in the fall of 1938, Rivera seems to finally have found out about the Trotsky-Kahlo affair, perhaps from Frida's sister Cristina herself. As a result, relations between the two men soured, even though Rivera never directly confronted Trotsky about the affair. Instead he accused Trotsky of obscure doctrinal transgressions and quit the Fourth International. Trotsky was put on notice that he should begin looking for a new place to stay.

In April 1939 Trotsky finally found a new hideout, a dark and cold bunker of a house on Avenida Viena, only six blocks from the Blue House. He had a wall built to surround the property and guardtowers erected to watch over the street. But none of this could protect him from the Stalinist noose that was tightening around his neck. After the defeat of Republican forces in Spain, Mexico opened its gates to thousands of war refugees, among them Tina Modotti and her lover Vittorio Vidali, Rivera's old nemesis from the Comintern who almost certainly had a hand in planning Trotsky's demise.

On May 24, 1940, a twenty-man team of assassins that included David Alfaro Siquieros appeared at the gates of Trotsky's fortress in the uniforms of Mexican policemen. One of the team was known to the guard, an American Trotskyite named Robert Harte. Harte was tricked into opening the steel gate and the team rushed in, firing hundreds of rounds of machine-gun fire into Trotsky's bedroom and studio. Miraculously, Trotsky and his wife saved themselves by jumping under their bed. Harte's body was found a week later in a field outside Mexico City. He had been murdered with a single shot to the back of the head, Vittorio Vidal's trademark. The job of killing Trotsky was successfully concluded on August 20 when another Stalinist agent named Ramon Mercader talked his way into Trotsky's office and buried an ice pick in Trotsky's head as "the old man" sat at his desk reading a political tract.

Frida doesn't seem to have experienced much grief when she heard of Trotsky's death. She immediately phoned Rivera, who had fled in fear to San Francisco after the first assassination attempt. "They killed Trotsky this morning," she said. "*Estupido!* It's your fault that they killed him. Why did you bring him [here]?"

Because she had met the assassin Mercader in Paris and had seen him again when he arrived in Mexico City, Frida was picked up by the police and interrogated for a day. But the police had nothing that would link her to the crime. Mercader was working as a deep-cover operative. He passed himself off as a Trotskyite, and the police didn't discover his real identity until almost ten years later. Frida had merely been a pawn in a dangerous global political game.

The Trotsky episode should have alerted Frida that she was treading in deep political waters and was in far over her head in her dealings with the Communist party. In the Soviet Union, monstrous crimes were being committed in the name of the proletariat. Evidence of these crimes was already clearly visible even by the late 1930s, but Frida didn't want to know about it. Communism, even if for the moment that didn't include the Communist party, was her faith. All those who spoke out against it were either liars or dupes, or traitors.

7

The Pseudo-Amateur

I have painted about twelve paintings, all small
and unimportant, with the same personal subjects that only
appeal to myself and nobody else.

—Frida Kahlo

BY 1938 FRIDA KAHLO had been painting in earnest for ten years. In that time she had completed around a dozen paintings that were of the highest caliber, works so original and compelling that they could have held their own with any of her contemporaries in the world. Yet she still hadn't had a single show of her paintings, and she had acquired only a few collectors, at least one of whom, Leo Eloesser, came by her works as barter items in payment for medical services. In fact, Frida was as apt to give her paintings away as she was to sell them (as she had done with Alejandro Gómez Arias and Leon Trotsky).

All signs indicate that Frida knew she was breaking exciting new ground with her work. Her fascinating synthesis of personal mythology, with folk art idioms, of dreamlike composition and darkly realistic subject matter was utterly new. Being an avid student of art history and of the work of her peers in Mexico, Europe, and the United States, she knew that she was onto something different. Yet she presented herself as an amateur, one without ambitions and who didn't take her own art seriously.

Her greatest supporter and admirer was her husband. Diego

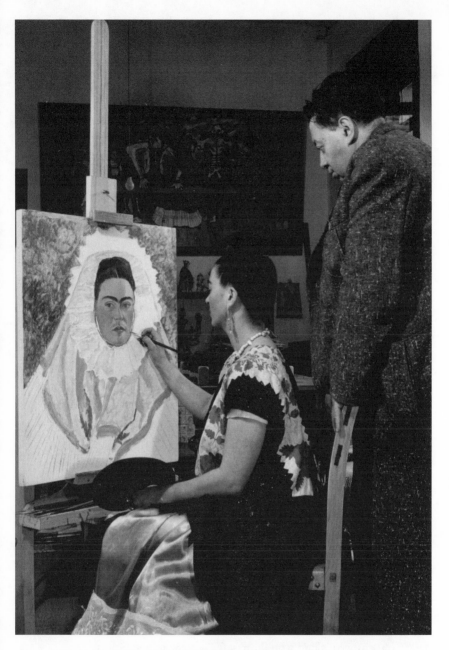

Frida paints Self-Portrait as a Tehuana, 1940.

Rivera wasn't known for being especially generous in his praise of his peers, but he always commended Frida's work and encouraged her to keep painting. It could be argued that this was a sign that Rivera didn't really consider Frida an equal as an artist or to be working at his level, that his support of Frida was patronizing and insincere. This argument doesn't do justice either to that part of him that was truly generous or to his actual intent. It was Diego in Cuernavaca, soon after they had married, who urged her to keep painting and had asked her opinion of the composition and color of the mural he was painting at the Cortés Palace. Later, as she lay disconsolate in her recovery at the *Henry Ford Hospital*, it was Diego who suggested that she take up a brush and paint images from her life. However single-mindedly self-involved he might have been in other parts of his life, Rivera was genuinely intrigued and impressed by Frida Kahlo's artistic vision and was a serious champion of her work.

At the very beginning of 1938, at the age of thirty-one, Frida, at Diego's urging, participated in her first show, a group exhibition at a small gallery near the University of Mexico. It was, Frida said, "a small and rotten place, but the only one that admits any kind of stuff . . . I send [my paintings] there without any kind of enthusiasm."

In spite of her protests, Frida must have enjoyed seeing her paintings hanging on the wall of a public space for the first time. Given her seeming lack of interest in her own career, she wasn't very good as a promoter of her own work. She fretted over her prices, almost felt sorry when someone paid for one of her paintings, and insisted that if somebody bought her work it must have been "because he's in love with me."

Nonetheless, after her sojourns in New York in 1933 and 1935, Frida's name had begun to circulate in the small Manhattan art world. In early 1938, she received a letter from Julien Levy, an enthusiast for modern art who had opened a small gallery on East Fifty-seventh Street in the early 1930s. Levy had eclectic and adventurous tastes, having first shown the photographers Eugène Atget and Man Ray before taking on many of the leading European Surrealists—Max Ernst, Salvador Dali, Giorgio de Chirico, and others—as well as a few Americans such as Alexander Calder and Joseph Cornell. According to Frida, "Somebody had talked [to Levy] about my paintings, and he [is] very much interested in having an exhibition in his gallery." Frida finished her comments by again denigrating herself: "I don't know what they see in my work. Why do they want me to have a show?"[1]

Unlike Rivera's enthusiasm for her work, Frida's modesty was a front she used to hide her insecurities about her vocation as an artist. It was easier to pretend that she wasn't serious about her work than it was to boldly step into the arts arena and possibly have her work attacked or dismissed. Frida also wasn't used to having the spotlight shine on her alone. At thirty-one, she had always operated as Diego Rivera's junior partner.

Even in terms of providing for her own living, she depended on Diego. Because she had sold very few paintings for little money, she hadn't come close to making a living selling her art; indeed she hadn't made a living at anything. Rivera paid all the bills. He had picked up all of her medical costs that were not bartered by paintings, all the day-to-day expenses, travel costs, the entire cost of their San Angel dwellings as well as the cost for the Blue House in Coyoacán, whose mortgage he paid off soon after he married Frida. Not being one to grumble about money, Diego had assumed these obligations willingly. But it left Frida in his debt, psychologically as well as financially, and especially after Diego's affair with her sister, Frida now wanted at the very least to be financially independent of her husband.

In spite of the continual protestations she made about Rivera's genius and her insignificance, in the early 1930s Frida had begun making choices that separated her work from her husband's. Her paintings were usually quite small, typically a foot by a foot and a half. They drew heavily on folkloric motifs such as the *retablos* and the lithographs of José Posada. They were often painted on the cheapest possible material, tin. There was a political reckoning in these choices. The tin, the echoes of the *retablos*, aligned Frida with Mexican popular culture, the art of "the people." If Rivera stood for monumental, accessible, very public work, she would define herself by being his opposite: work that was small in scale, whose content was more enigmatic, and which was executed, and until 1938 held, in private.

Even though she felt the need to hide her ambition behind the mask of the "occasional painter" and the painter of the "exotic," underneath this camouflage was an artist whose work gives powerful testimony to her intent and ambition in her desire to be known and respected. Frida's outward attitude toward her work was strictly pose.

This false modesty notwithstanding, Frida would make an appearance in the world in 1938. She sent photos of her work to Julien Levy, and they agreed on a one-woman show, another first for her, at his gallery in late November. In April, the man known as the "pope of Surrealism" landed in Mexico. André Breton was intent on seeing Mexican culture firsthand and also meeting with his political hero, Leon Trotsky. He also would cast his jaundiced eye at the Mexican art scene to see if its participants came up to his exacting standards of political correctness, personal style, and willingness to agree with his point of view.

Breton considered himself the founder and leader of Surrealism, a vanity that doesn't match up with the historical record or how the ideas in this constellation moved from one artist to another in the years during and after the First World War. In 1928, he wrote in his manifesto, *Surrealism and Painting:*

> I am very lenient. So long as an artist's work or life does not sink into general confusion, and so long as abysmally mean and low considerations do not end up outweighing all other factors that might otherwise persuade me that the life or the work in question is truly significant and exemplary, I ask nothing than to give praise and respect where it is due.

By which he meant—to André Breton—which the poets Antonin Artaud and Robert Desnos and artist Salvador Dali found out at various times when Breton decided that they had sunk into "general confusion" and publicly banished them from the movement.

Breton and his wife Jacqueline spent most of their several months in Mexico at Diego and Frida's San Angel home/studios, from which they, often with Trotsky, made excursions into the Mexican countryside. Frida quickly found out that Breton was a pompous bore and generally tried to stay away from him as much as possible. She found Jacqueline to have a much more quick and fluid imagination than her husband. Soon the two of them formed a kind of informal alliance against the trio of overbearing, dogmatic men.

In spite of being shunted aside, André Breton was captivated by Frida and her work. He promised to try to arrange a show for her in Paris that would coincide with her forthcoming show in New York and to write a piece about her for the New York show and as publicity for Paris. With his typical brand of self-referential praise, he wrote:

> My surprise and joy were unbounded when I discovered, on

my arrival in Mexico, that her work has blossomed forth, in her latest paintings, into pure surreality, despite the fact that it had been conceived without any prior knowledge whatsoever of the ideas motivating the activities of my friends and myself. . . . I was witnessing here, at the other end of the earth, a spontaneous outpouring of our own questioning spirit.[2]

Then, to acknowledge Frida's luck at living with Rivera and having met him, Breton added: "We are privileged to be present . . . at the entry of a young woman endowed with all the gifts of seduction, one accustomed to the society of men of genius."

Later that summer, Frida met up with a much more known, but more self-effacing celebrity. On a vacation to Mexico City, the tough-guy actor Edward G. Robinson stopped by the Rivera-Kahlo compound. Robinson was a considerable art collector and had come to buy some of Rivera's paintings. While Gladys Robinson, Edward's wife, was on the rooftop talking with Frida, Rivera pulled out some of Frida's canvases, which she had hidden away. Robinson was so taken with them that he immediately bought four for two hundred dollars each. Frida was elated when she learned about the sales. "This way I am going to be free. I'll be able to travel and do what I want without asking Diego for money."

In a buoyant mood, Frida left Mexico in October for New York. As in 1935, she was traveling alone, leaving *panzón* to his compulsive habits in Mexico City. Rivera did pause long enough to help pave Frida's way to New York. He had got in touch with artists, dealers, collectors, and museum curators to let them know about her show and provided her with an even more extensive list of people to contact when she got to New York. Bertram Wolfe, Rivera's old Central Committee comrade—now a nonparty fellow traveler and working on a biography of

Rivera—had been dispatched to write an article about Frida in *Vanity Fair*. For a self-proclaimed amateur, Frida, with Rivera's help, managed to mount an impressive publicity campaign.

The show, which included twenty-five of her paintings, opened on November 1. It garnered generally good, if superficial reviews in the press. *Time* magazine, referring to Frida as "little Frida," called the show "the flutter of the week" in its Art section and opined that Frida's work had "the playfully bloody fancy of an unsentimental child."[3]

The paintings sold fairly well, especially considering that the show occurred during the Great Depression. About half of the work was purchased, although some, like the ones that belonged to Edward G. Robinson, had been sold before the show began.

Frida's Communist scruples about "rich guys here . . . having parties day and night while . . . people are dying of hunger," so visible in 1933, seem to have died out completely by 1938. In fact, her stay in New York was one long schmooze with rich patrons and potential patrons. She lunched with Clare Booth Luce, playwright, editor of *Vanity Fair*, and wife of Henry Luce, owner of the *Time* magazine empire. She painted a copy of *Fulang-Chang and I*, a self-portrait of herself and her favorite pet monkey (which had been sold to another collector), for Conger Goodyear, president of the Museum of Modern Art. She spent a week at the famous and recently built house in Pennsylvania of Edgar J. Kaufmann (Fallingwater, designed by Frank Lloyd Wright), who had bought one of her paintings from the Levy Gallery. And most astonishing of all, she buried the hatchet with Nelson Rockefeller, whom she previously had demonized as the essence of capitalist depravity when Rivera's Rockefeller Center mural was destroyed.

Frida also had time for New York City street life and popular culture. She loved visiting Chinatown and exploring Manhattan shop windows for inexpensive curiosities. She also took the opportunity to catch up on American movies. During her trip to New York in 1933, she had developed a taste for American comedies and horror films. Her favorites were the Marx Brothers, the Three Stooges, and Frankenstein, which she saw several times.

The 1938–39 stay in New York was probably the most relaxed and enjoyable trip she ever took outside her country—and in a way that had nothing to do with her career. During these days in New York, she fell in love, and for the first and last time, seems to have considered the possibility of leaving Diego Rivera.

The man to whom Frida became so ardently attached was the portrait and fashion photographer Nickolas Muray. Muray had immigrated to America from Hungary in 1913 when he was twenty-one years old. Starting with nothing, he managed through talent and personal charm to carve out a niche for himself as a photographer. By the late twenties, his photos were appearing regularly in magazines such as *Harper's Bazaar* and *Vanity Fair*.

Frida had first met Muray in Mexico in the mid-1930s. They may have begun a casual affair then, but by the time Frida left New York for Paris in January 1939, their relationship had blossomed into a full-blown romance. From Paris she wrote him, "I miss every movement of your being, your voice, your eyes, your hands, your beautiful mouth. . . . YOU. I love you my Nick. I am so happy to think that I love you—to think that you wait for me—you love me." Hoping for an extended stay with Muray, Frida decided that she would return from Paris to New York, not Mexico City.

Frida also wrote Rivera from Paris, but increasingly her letters to him, and later her references to him in her diary, have the feel of a ritualized liturgy. Rather than addressing herself to an actual man, she seems to be offering prayers to a minor deity, a talisman who must be remembered lest isolation, loneliness, and a vague but poisonous fear descend on her:

> It is six in the morning
> and the turkeys are singing.
> heat of human tenderness
> Solitude accompanied—
> Never in all my life
> will I forget your presence
> You picked me up when I was destroyed
> and you made me whole again. . . .
> Do not stop giving thirst
> to the tree of which you are the sun, the tree
> that treasured your seed
> "Diego" is the name of love.[4]

Frida arrived in Paris in January 1939 to find that the show that André Breton was supposedly organizing for her was a mess. "The gallery was not arranged for the exhibit at all," Frida wrote Nickolas Muray in her colloquial English (which gives an idea of her everyday style of speech in Spanish),

> and Breton has no gallery of his own. So I had to wait days and days just like an idiot till I met Marcel Duchamp . . . who is the only one who had his feet on the earth, among all this bunch of coocoo lunatic sons of bitches of the surrealists. . . . Now Breton wants to exhibit together with my paintings, 14 portraits of the XIX century, . . . 32 photographs of Alvarez Bravo, and lots of popular objects which he bought on the markets of Mexico—*all this junk*—can you beat that?

The show, which had begun as a showcase for Frida only, finally opened at a small Paris gallery in March. As Frida had feared, it now had turned into a confusing collection of Mexicana, rather than an exhibition of the works of Frida Kahlo, and featured Breton's "junk" as well as nineteenth-century *retablos* and Manuel Avarez Bravo's photos. Further, she didn't sell anything. On March 25, she set sail for Nick Muray and New York, and bid good-bye to the art world of Paris, which

> [made] me vomit. They are so damned "intellectual" and rotten that I can't stand them any more. . . . I'd rather sit on the floor in the market of Toluca and sell tortillas than to have any thing to do with these "artistic" bitches of Paris. They sit for hours on the "cafes" . . . and talk without stopping about "culture" "art" "revolution," . . . dreaming the most fantastic nonsense and poisoning the air with theories that never come true. . . . I will hate this place and its people for as long as I live. There is something so false and unreal about them that they drive me nuts.

Frida returned to New York to find that her relationship with Nickolas Muray had turned sour. In her absence, Muray had begun a relationship with a woman he would marry in June. The suddenness of the reversal of her romance with Muray hit Frida hard and caused her to leave New York much sooner than she had planned. By early May 1939 she was back in Mexico City, but it is clear from a flurry of letters between her and Muray that she still was sorting out the failed relationship that summer.

"When I received your letter, a few days ago," Frida wrote Muray in June, "I didn't know what to do. I must tell you that I couldn't help weeping. I felt that something was in my throat, just as if I had swallowed the whole world. I don't know yet if I was sad, jealous or angry, but the sensation I felt was in the first place of great despair."[5]

The end of the relationship with Muray wasn't simply the

The Two Fridas, 1939.

end of a love affair. It also marked the end of Frida's attempt to escape from the entrapment of her "common vision" with Diego Rivera. This common vision was all encompassing; it included agreements about a shared outlook in politics, approaches to art, and explicit and implicit rules of conduct for daily life, the last a framework that Frida must have found suffocating by 1939.[6]

By linking up with Muray, Frida could have taken her life in an entirely new direction. Her art certainly would have changed because her life with Muray would have been hugely different than the life she was leading with Rivera. But most important, she seems to have been looking for an emotional constancy that was absent in her relationship with Rivera. Her breakup with Muray is made all the more poignant because of how it reveals this intense emotional need.

Back in Mexico, Frida found herself locked into a pattern that, in the tantalizing light of what might have been with Nick Muray no longer made sense. Yet she was stuck; she didn't have the nerve to break with Diego, and there was no other person who had the charisma to entice her away. In July she either moved out, or was asked by Diego to move out, of the San Angel studio. But this time instead of taking an apartment in central Mexico City she moved back into the Blue House. In September, she and Rivera filed for a divorce, which was granted in December.

The divorce seems to have been instigated by Rivera, although why he should suddenly want a divorce in 1939 is not clear. He offered an entirely self-serving excuse in his autobiography. "I never was a faithful husband," he wrote, ". . . I loved [Frida] too much to want to cause her suffering, and to spare her further torments, I decided to separate from her." In fact, he probably found out about Frida's affair with Muray. The depth of her feelings for Muray could easily have dented Rivera's weak ego. The price he extracted was a divorce. Frida, who preferred the familiarity of the status quo to the unknown of a life without Diego, weakly objected, but soon gave her consent.

During the fall of 1939, Frida again fell ill. She developed fungal infections in her right hand and experienced shooting pains in her spine. Her newest doctor, Juan Farill of Mexico City, advised complete bed rest and rigged up a particularly nasty-looking, spine-stretching contraption, a forty-pound weight, looped around her head and to which she was married for hours each day.

During this physical and emotional torture, Frida continued to work on a painting she had begun in September, an allegory of her life called *The Two Fridas*. Measuring six and one half feet square, the painting is much larger than her usual work. Also, unlike many of her previous works, this painting is neither executed on tin, nor borrows iconography from folk sources. Instead it is painted on canvas and shows two Frida Kahlos sitting on a bench and holding hands. One Frida is wearing a white, lacy dress. Around the heart, the blouse magically disintegrates to show a heart eaten away and seemingly diseased. The other Frida, who wears a Tehuana outfit, also displays her heart, which appears healthy. In her hand she holds a tiny photograph of Diego Rivera as a boy. A slender vein runs between the two women and ends in the lap of the white-dressed Frida, who clamps it shut with surgical pincers. Blood still leaks from the vein onto the clean white dress. Even some of the flower and bird designs at the dress's hemline have transformed into bloodstains.

Frida told a visitor at the time she completed the painting that the Tehuana Frida is the one loved by Diego Rivera. The other, white-clad-Frida, had been scorned by Rivera. (The visitor, American art historian MacKinley Helm, also reported that Frida had doubts whether "her career would prosper, apart from him," a very unsentimental assessment of Rivera's worth as a husband.) Thus the painting is clearly a statement by Frida about the way she perceived herself during the time of her divorce.

Yet, in spite of her continuing protestations of love for Rivera, there is no feeling for Rivera in this painting. Instead the painting is about Frida Kahlo and her intolerable sense of alienation. In the painting Rivera is seen as an icon, a child in a photograph contained within a locket. In the same way that Frida uses Diego as a symbol for her unquenchable need for human contact in her letters and diary, she also encapsulates him within the locket as a symbol for something much larger than the flesh and blood man. He is the demon/deity/vessel by which and through which she fends off her intolerable sense of separation and loneliness.

Self-Portrait with Cropped Hair, 1940.

8

On Her Own Terms

Work: I organize things as necessary to live more or less "decently." . . .
[and] have my afternoons free to spend on the beautiful art of painting.
I'm always painting pictures, since as soon as I'm done with one,
I have to sell it so I have moola for all of the month's expenses.

—*Frida Kahlo*

AFTER HER DIVORCE, Frida began working hard to try to support herself financially. In a letter to Nickolas Muray, she swore, "I don't accept a damned cent from Diego, the reasons you must understand. I will never accept money from any man till I die."

Her expenses weren't terribly large. Thanks to Rivera's generosity, the Blue House was paid for. And in spite of her protestations, a fair portion of her day-to-day expenses were covered by Rivera too, although this money came to her in a way that allowed her to plead ignorance of its source.

Frida and Diego had rigged up a convoluted banking system that was handled through Alberto Misrachi, owner of a popular bookstore in Mexico City. Misrachi was also a collector of their art as well as their part-time dealer. He handled their finances, clearing checks given to them for their art and lending them money during dry spells. Frida frequently asked him for advances, which were drawn mostly on sales of Rivera's work.

Even though she was still financially beholden to Rivera and would continue to be for the rest of her life, in 1940 Frida began to sell more of her work, which gave her the comforting illusion that she was financially self-sufficient. She solicited portrait commissions from her collectors, especially the Mexican diplomat Eduardo Morillo Safa and the engineer José Domingo Lavin. And she also managed to sell self-portraits, a form that appealed to her aesthetic sensibilities and for which she would become well known.

Between 1940 and 1945, Frida painted at least ten self-portraits (twelve if one includes paintings in which she appears but is not the central subject). A typical Kahlo self-portrait is a close-up of her head and shoulders in which she is facing the viewer. Usually her head is turned slightly left or right, although a few show her looking straight ahead. She never smiles, but always is portrayed with an expressionless, sometimes even severe, visage.

These self-portraits are not meant to show the woman that one would have encountered in everyday life: the witty, wisecracking, often foul-mouthed Frida, defiant of conventional morality, or the tender and solicitous friend or children's mother figure. Instead we come face to face with a mask, a severe, almost haughty and removed persona who would not look out of place in eighteenth-century French court paintings.

One of the reasons for the unsmiling face can be traced back to Frida's addiction to sweets. As a result of her sweet tooth and poor dental care, many of her teeth were rotten. She did have some false teeth, but according to her friends, felt self-conscious about smiling. Thus, what could be interpreted as coldness in her photos and self-portraits is at least partially an acute and awkward self-consciousness about her smile.

The American arts writer Parker Leslie told an amusing story about Frida's teeth and how it could affect her personality. Once in the mid-1940s, he accompanied Frida to a dance performance at the Palacio de Bellas Artes in downtown Mexico City. Fashionably late, she and Leslie entered the hall:

[Suddenly] no one paid any attention to the dance performance. . . . Everyone stared at Frida, who wore her Tehuana
dress and all of Diego's gold jewelry, and clanked like a knight
in armor. She had the Byzantine opulence of the Empress
Theodora, a combination of barbarism and elegance. She had
two gold incisors and when she was all gussied up she would
take off the plain gold caps and put on gold caps with rose
diamonds in front, so her smile really sparkled.[1]

The unsmiling Fridas of the self-portraits have been interpreted
as revealing a passive or stoic sufferer, and it is primarily from
these self-portraits that the idea of Kahlo the Sufferer and Kahlo
the Victim has arisen. These interpretations of Frida and her
work are only partially correct. A look at the iconography that
Frida uses in these paintings is useful in deciphering any messages she may have intended for her audience.

Some of the iconographic messages she presents in the self-
portraits are obvious. For instance, in two of the self-portraits,
tears leak from the corners of her eyes, a clear sign of sadness or
distress. In two other self-portraits she has inscribed images in the
center of her forehead, her "third-eye" spot. These clearly indicate to the viewer what she has been thinking about—in one death
is indicated by skull and bones, in another Diego Rivera is shown.

However, other bits of iconography are more subtle. In two
self-portraits, she wears a bramble necklace whose thorns prick
her skin. This "crown of thorns" is directly borrowed from the
numerous and bloody Crucifixion images depicted in Mexican
colonial art, but cleverly Frida has placed this garland not as a
crown but, appropriate for a woman, as a necklace. The necklace
is an adornment, possibly given to her by a husband or lover. But
this adornment is double-sided; it shows off the beauty of her

slender neck even as it imprisons and pricks her. The implications of her acceptance of the necklace bind her. As a symbol of oppressive tradition, it is sublime.

Animals—monkeys, cats, parrots, hummingbirds, and the Mexican hairless dog called the Itzcuintli that Frida was fond of—appear in six paintings. These animals show us a part of Frida's domestic life. She kept all of the animals at various times. Her favorite monkey was a Mexican spider monkey named Caimito de Guayabal, and she kept a parrot in the courtyard of the Blue House that liked to drink tequila and shriek, "*No me pasa la cruda!*" (I can't get over this hangover!). However, some of the animals also stand in as symbols for Frida's feelings. In two of these paintings, ribbons loop from around Frida's neck to the animals, indicating a special bond between her and them. Her pets were to her a kind of family; they filled in for the children she could never have and they offered familiar comfort in a world she felt increasingly alienated from.

Frida tapped Mexican pre-Colombian mythology to express feelings and urges through these animals. In preconquest Mexico, the monkey was a symbol of sexual desire; the hummingbird, which in another self-portrait hangs dead from a thorny necklace, symbolized luck in love. Because the hummingbird was dead, Frida was signaling her amorous misfortunes.

In all but one of the self-portraits, Frida is wearing Tehuana dress. She would assume and cast off Tehuana clothing as she clung to or was cast off by Rivera. Most of the self-portraits in which she portrays herself in Tehuana costume were painted after she had remarried Diego late in 1940.

Frida painted two very different self-portraits in 1940. The first is not the standard kind just described, rather it is more a dreamscape in which she has imagined herself as part of the dream.

This painting, straightforwardly called *The Dream*, conveys the immediacy of her emotions at the time of her divorce. On the most immediate level, it expresses her preoccupation with death—the ultimate form of alienation from the world of human passions. Frida, as imagined by her self, lies asleep on a canopied bed, dreaming within a dream. A vine grows at her feet and entwines around the blanket that covers her body. Atop the canopy lies her twin—death—in the form of a Judas figure popular in Mexican folk mythology.

Frida takes an unexpected leap by using the Judas in this painting. She was fond of folkloric artifacts such as this and for a while actually kept the Judas shown in this painting atop her own bed. Mexicans burn Judases on Sábado de Gloria, the Saturday before Easter, as a way to seek vengeance on and symbolically rid themselves of those who oppress them—especially politicians, landlords, police, and generals. Often these Judases are caricatures of living persons, a particularly rapacious and despised president for instance. The Judas is another embodiment of the phenomenon of *chingada*; it is the Judas who has "screwed" the people. One turn-of-the-century observer described how these effigies were treated by crowds on Tacuba Street in central Mexico City:

> [Judases] stretched on wires . . . from one house to the other were bright-colored, hideous figures, representing the maldito [accursed one] dangling in grotesque attitudes against the blue sky. On various street corners he is burned in effigy. Firecrackers are exploding . . . bells are ringing from every belfry. Grief is noisy in the tropics. . . . [As the figures burned] many people were wrought up to a pitch of religious frenzy, and if an arm or leg was thrown off intact, they seized and tore it with their teeth.[2]

The Dream, 1940.

There is a deeper interpretation of the identity of the Judas who sleeps with Frida in *The Dream*. He is death, of course, but he is also Diego Rivera, the betrayer.

The second of Frida's 1940 self-portraits is also unlike the standard version of her earlier works, but not because it is a dream. Instead it is shockingly realistic, yet of a kind of heightened realism, like a victim often feels after a physical confrontation or attack: reality under the influence of adrenaline. It is another divorce-period painting, entitled *Self-Portrait with Cropped Hair*, and shows Frida dressed in a baggy suit, simple shirt, and men's lace shoes. The size of the suit indicates that it could have been one of Diego's. She holds a pair of scissors in her lap and her hair is cropped short. Long strands of shorn hair seem to float in the space surrounding her. Written above the painting are the words of a popular Mexican song: "Look, if I loved you, it was for your hair. Now that you are bald, I don't love you anymore."

As always, Frida was "painting her life." She actually did cut her hair during this time. In a letter to Nick Muray, she said that she looked "just like a ferry [fairy]." She is clearly rejecting standard ideals of femininity; it is as if she is lashing out at Rivera for his rejection of her. However, as usually happens in one of her paintings, the visual information presented by Frida is clear yet not belabored. The viewer is at first sent reeling by an almost violent image of a woman shorn of her hair, then is left intrigued by the ambiguous clues in the painting. One of the most subtle of these ciphers is the color of the upper background, a nauseating greenish yellow gray. In her diary Frida explained her interpretation of various colors; one of these was "GREENISH YELLOW: more madness and mystery. All the phantoms wear suits of this color."

Anger rather than suffering or sadness is the sensibility expressed in *Self-Portrait with Cropped Hair.* However, the other self-portraits play on the latter themes. The iconography of a few of the paintings—*The Two Fridas*, the self-portraits with the thorn necklaces, the tear-stained self-portrait with Diego in her "third-eye"—do suggest that Frida is trying to portray herself as a passive victim. Yet most of the others are more subtle evocations of a diffuse pain, or an almost cosmic or fated state of isolation that no number of burning Judases will assuage. The emotional candor, the brazenness, the hauteur, the tears dripping from the eyes, the companionship of animals and not of humans all speak of a vast, unshakable loneliness: a perception on the part of the artist that she has failed to connect with the world but cannot put her finger on why that is. No matter that most of this isolation may have been masochistic or self-imposed, it is nonetheless real. Frida's fierce originality and genius shines through in her ability to capture this sensibility in a spellbinding and subtlety changing way. Her self-portraits capture in the visual medium what the playwright James Saunders has described in his play *Next Time I'll Sing to You:*

> There lies behind everything, and you can believe this or not as you wish, a certain quality which we may call grief. It's always there, just under the surface, just behind the facade, sometimes very nearly exposed, so that you can dimly see the shape of it as you can see sometimes through the surface of an ornamental pond on a still day, the dark, gross, inhuman outline of a carp gliding slowly past; when you suddenly realize that the carp were always there beneath the surface, even while the water sparkled in the sunshine.

In May 1940, after the first, unsuccessful assassination attempt on Leon Trotsky, Diego Rivera decided his life was in danger and began making plans to flee Mexico. Even though he had been a Trotskyite, Rivera knew that the Mexican government wanted to question him about the Trotsky incident (some government officials thought Rivera may have turned on Trotsky and set up the assassination attempt). The government had already arrested muralist David Alfaro Siquieros for his presumed role in the attack, but Siquieros was a well-known Stalinist and thus had a clear motive to try to kill Trotsky. Still, Rivera wasn't popular with the police and government security agents; he was afraid of being framed or held for months without being formally charged with a crime.

Rivera was smuggled out of his San Angel studio to a hiding place by his girlfriend, screen actress Paulette Goddard. He then contacted the American embassy to get help in leaving the country. United States immigration officials facilitated Rivera's quick entry into the United States. A communiqué marked "strictly confidential" from the embassy in Mexico City to the State Department on May 31, 1940, stated that, "Mr. Rivera is undoubtably seriously disturbed by the police investigations and desires to go to the United States immediately. Mr. Rivera applied for and has been issued a border identification card in order that there will be no delay in identifying him at the border."[3] On June 3, a terse telegraph from the embassy to Washington reported, "Diego Rivera departs Mexico City by airplane June 4, 7:45 a.m. via Brownsville, final destination San Francisco."

Rivera was able to receive the prompt and personal attention of the U.S. embassy because since January he had been an informant for them about the activities of his one-time comrades in the Mexican Communist party. In the years since Rivera's return to Mexico, old allies in the struggle for revolutionary arts had gone their separate ways in choosing international causes and allies. Dr. Atl, for instance, although still a personal friend of Rivera's was now a fascist sympathizer. Rivera, on the other hand, had managed to convince himself that "every effort should be made toward cooperation between the United States and Latin America" to defeat the fascist threat in Europe.

In January Rivera had met with Robert McGregor, an embassy consular officer. During the meeting, which occurred at Rivera's studio in San Angel, Rivera gave his views about the aims of the Mexican Communist party, tipped off American agents about Spanish Communists who had come to Mexico after the end of the Spanish Civil War, and told them about a meeting between a Mexican Communist leader and John L. Lewis, head of the U.S. labor organization, Congress of Industrial Organizations. A memorandum extracting the crucial points of this conversation was forwarded back to Washington with the observation that "in view of Rivera's known tendency towards exaggeration, if not even fabrication, many of the statements should . . . be accepted with considerable reserve." Nonetheless, the embassy appreciated Rivera's cooperation and helped him quickly get out of Mexico.

It is extremely unlikely that Frida knew about Rivera's double-dealing stratagems with the U.S. embassy. Frida had been and was still in 1940 deeply involved with an organization that aided refugees from the Spanish Civil War. It is likely that some of the names that Rivera handed over to the U.S. embassy were of people whom Frida knew personally. Rivera must have comforted himself with the idea that his treachery wouldn't result in any harm to those he had exposed, and probably he was right about this. Still, this incident illuminates the shallowness of his politics; stripped bare of empty "revolutionary" rhetoric, Rivera can clearly be seen as an opportunist.

To avoid his enemies real and imagined, Rivera accepted a

Dr. Atl: Artist, Volcanologist, Provocateur

Of all the artists who made names for themselves in early-twentieth-century Mexico, few are more fascinating and contrary than Gerardo Murillo, better known by his pseudonym Dr. Atl, the shadowy, devious, and unpredictable godfather of Mexican revolutionary art.

Born in 1875 in Mexico's second city, Guadalajara, Murillo was of the generation that immediately preceded Diego Rivera into the world of Mexican arts. An erratic and rebellious student, he left his native city for the capital in 1894, where equally erratically he studied art at the San Carlos Academy, then the major arts college in Mexico. He somehow managed to hustle a grant from the government of Porfirio Díaz for studies abroad and left Mexico for Europe in 1896. For seven years he knocked around Spain, France, and Italy, absorbing its bohemian attitudes as much as its historical and contemporary visual art.

On his return to Mexico in 1903, Murillo decided that his name was insufficiently Mexican, so he changed it to Dr. Atl. The honorary doctorate in philosophy and penal administration that Murillo claimed was apparently self-rewarded for there is no evidence in the archives of French or Spanish universities that indicate degrees given to the peripatetic Mexican. The "Atl" part of his name he borrowed from Nahuatl, the language of the Aztecs and other peoples of central Mexico. It is the word for *water* and symbolically allied Murillo with Choc, the Aztec god of water and life. To further solidify his Mexicanness, Atl claimed to have swam in all of the rivers in Mexico, literally baptizing himself in his nation's streams. Thus a Mexican nationalist was born.

By 1904–05 Atl was teaching art at the San Carlos Academy, the same time that Diego Rivera was finishing his studies there. Atl's self-mythologizing and knowledge of contemporary European art (especially Cezanne, then unknown in Mexico) entranced the young Rivera, and the two men were to remain close throughout their lives. Atl was also apparently a disruptive influence at the academy.

Around 1908, Atl developed a fascination for volcanoes, especially Popocatépetl, the magnificent, dormant, snow-capped peak that, in the days before Mexico City became a soup bowl for some of the worst pollution in the world, could clearly be seen from the city. He spent a year on the mountainside, painting the peak over and over again, and in later years painted and studied volcanoes in Mexico, Italy, and Japan. Nothing better cured the sickness of the soul, he later would write, "than the zero-degree air and ice at the peak of a volcano."

Before 1910, Atl had been generally disengaged from politics. But during the Revolution, Atl temporarily abandoned his art career for politics. During the short-lived presidency of insurgent general Venustiano Carranza, he organized so-called "red battalions" of workers, primarily from Mexico City, to battle Carranza foes such as Pancho Villa. He also worked behind the scenes as a propagandist and special agent for Carranza. However, Atl's patronage and money were cut off when Carranza was overthrown by one of his top generals, Alvaro Obregón, in 1919.

Unfortunately, both Atl's politics and art were unstable and in the end unfruitful. He never managed to break free of eccentric projects such as capturing the "spirits" of volcanoes through painting. In politics, he was at best an opportunist who flowed with what he thought was a winning tide. This lack of scruples, coupled with a touchy sense of nationalism, led him to become

an enthusiastic supporter of German and Italian fascism in 1930s and early 1940s. In siding with the fascists, Dr. Atl was extending his appreciation for political strongmen to a global level. He also saw the Germans and Italians as a counterweight to the power of the United States, whose influence on Mexico Atl deplored.

Although Atl was not a particularly talented or interesting painter, he vigorously championed the new art and artists that arose in the aftermath of the Mexican Revolution. By 1919 he had finally become director of the San Carlos Academy and urged Mexico's new leaders to encourage a nationalist art that would blend Mexican themes with the style of public art seen in Italian renaissance frescoes. Atl also wrote a number of articles praising the murals of Diego Rivera, and later he became a fervent admirer of Frida Kahlo.

It is in this role of art promoter and champion of Mexico's arts heritage that Atl achieved real success. By encouraging Rivera, Kahlo, and other Mexican artists at various stages of their careers, Atl helped birth a nationalist, revolutionary Mexican art that at once acknowledged its European roots as it celebrated the Mexican national heritage.

Frida, Leon and Natalia Trotsky, and contingent of undercover
policemen at their arrival in Mexico City, 1937.

well-timed offer to paint a mural on the theme of Pan-American Unity for the Golden Gate Exposition in San Francisco. This also put him closer to two of his main paramours of the time, Paulette Goddard and his studio assistant Irene Brohus, who also had an apartment in San Francisco.

Even though he was divorced from Frida, Diego grew increasingly concerned for her safety and health in Mexico. He knew that she was only painting a few hours a day, that she was pinioned for further hours each day to Dr. Farill's spine-stretching machine, and that other medical consultants in Mexico had recommended that she undergo spinal surgery to correct "tuberculosis of the spine."

Diego contacted Dr. Eloesser in San Francisco who urged Frida to come see him before she embarked on any drastic medical procedures. Eloesser also counseled a reconciliation with Rivera who, Eloesser said, "loves you very much, and you love him. It is also the case, and you know it better than I, that besides you, he has two great loves— 1) Painting 2) Women in general. He has never been, nor will he ever be, monogamous, something that is imbecilic and anti-biological. Reflect, Frida, on this basis. What do you want to do?"

In September Frida flew to San Francisco. Eloesser performed a series of tests and quickly discovered that she wasn't suffering from any kind of bone ailment that required surgery but that she had developed a heavy dependence on tequila and brandy. He advised rest and total abstinence from alcohol. As it had in the past, Eloesser's cure worked; after a few weeks, Frida felt well enough to travel to New York to see Julien Levy and other friends.

While Frida was in New York, Eloesser continued to act as mediator and marriage counselor. He advised Rivera that Frida's health was faltering not because of any diseases but from "nerves" that were a result of her divorce. The only way for her to get better, Eloesser said, was for them to reunite. Rivera agreed and for once admitted that the separation was having a bad effect on him too. Still, Frida would not agree to remarriage on his first proposal. Her pride demanded that he ask her several times before she accepted. In the meanwhile she canvassed her friends about what she should do. One close friend, Anita Brenner cautioned against remarrying. In a letter she diagnosed Rivera as

> basically a sad person. He looks for warmth. . . . Naturally he looks for you. Although I am not really sure if he knows that you are the only one of all of them that really loved him. . . . It's natural to want to return to him, but I wouldn't do it, since what attracts Diego to you is what he doesn't have, and if he doesn't have you tied down completely, he will keep on looking for and needing you. . . . Do something with your own life; for that is what cushions us when the blows and falls come. . . . The blow is not as strong if there is something which allows us to say: Here I am, I am worth something. I am not so completely identified as someone else's shadow that when I cannot be in their shadow I am nothing.[4]

Frida's need to fill the loneliness inside herself was too great to remain single. She accepted Rivera's offer but according to him, with certain conditions: "she would provide for herself financially [more an illusion than a reality as has been shown]" and "we would have no sexual intercourse. [She said] that with the images of all my other women flashing through her mind, she couldn't possibly make love with me."[5]

In late November Frida flew back to San Francisco; on December 8, Diego's birthday, they were once again married, this time in San Francisco's Municipal Building. After a two-week stay with Diego in California, she returned alone to the Blue House to spend Christmas with her family.

Over the next four years, Frida's health fluxuated with events in her life and the world. He father's death in July 1941 was a blow that weakened her. Also the catastrophic war in Europe made her despair for the future. Her Communist ideals were clearly being threatened by fascism in Germany, Italy, and Japan. As usual, though, in politics she followed the lead of her shifty husband. After having vehemently rejected Soviet communism for years following his expulsion from the Communist party, and having snitched on the Party to the U.S. government later, Rivera gradually came to embrace Stalin as a powerful defender of Communist orthodoxy. Frida followed suit; by 1945, she would place Stalin along with Mao, Marx, and Lenin among her pantheon of all-male heroes. She would hang photographs of these men above her sickbed.

Mainly though, Frida tried to stay focused on her daily life. She fell into a habit of painting for a few hours in either the morning or the afternoon. Depending on what time she chose to paint, she would set aside the other part of the day to rest in the sun in the courtyard of the Blue House, visit her sisters, or go to the nearby Coyoacán market with friends. In the evenings, she would occasionally go into downtown Mexico City to hear mariachis sing at Garibaldi Plaza, or to attend dance and music performances.

From 1940 through 1944, her health was, at best steady, which is to say that it didn't get significantly worse. But she did-n't have much extra energy; walking quickly exhausted her and she had to carefully dole out time for work. In this way, she steadily and slowly painted self-portraits, still lifes, and commis-sioned portraits that provided her with a small, uneven income. But more than this, she laid out on canvas and tin a vision of one woman's life, a solitary struggle to understand herself in her own culture and in the world outside Mexico.

It wasn't Frida's style to strive for the heroic in her paintings. Her art was not about establishing new movements or proclaiming the role of the artist as cultural hero. Instead she held fast to an aesthetic of emotional openness in her art. Her paintings are pictorial constructions of her evolving self and her honesty about her fears and needs is what gives her efforts and works such poignancy.

Frida with her friend Teresa Proenza, 1952.

9

Death Is a Friend

I know how men must feed on barren hope.
—Aeschylus, Agamemnon

FRIDA HAD BEEN TEACHING for two years by 1945 at a place
called La Esmeralda, a secondary art school run by the Ministry
of Education. Her students were young, impressionable, working-class artists-in-training who came to La Esmeralda because
it was free. Frida had taken the job to draw a modest but regular salary. As a side benefit, the job would take her out of the soli-
tude of her house and into the world.

At first the students weren't sure what to think of her. None of
them knew who she was, and one of them, Fanny Rabel, recalled
that "in the beginning, when they told me that I was going to have
a woman teacher, I did not like the idea. It is an old vice of women
not to have confidence in women." Frida had met a female teacher
in the school's administrative office and news of the encounter had
leaked to the students. Frida had asked the other teacher, "What's
this about teaching? I don't know anything about teaching."[1] The
remark had made some of the students nervous.

As soon as they observed her in action, though, the students
grew to like and appreciate Frida. "The only help she gave us
was to stimulate us," a former student recalled about Frida's

151

teaching style. "She did not say even half a word about how we should paint, or anything about style. . . . She did not pretend to explain theoretical things. But she was enthusiastic about us." Another former student remembered that "Frida's greatest teaching was to see through artist's eyes, to open our eyes to see the world, to see Mexico. She did not influence us through her way of painting, but through her way of living." "Muchachos," she would announce,

"locked up here in school we can't do anything. Let's go into the street. Let's go and paint the life in the street."

By 1945, Frida had found the commute to the school building too taxing and asked her students to come instead to the Blue House in Coyoacán. At first most of her twenty or so students came to her house several times a week. Gradually the number dropped until at last only five or six came regularly. This dedicated group would come to be known as Los Fridos.

The sessions at her house were more like fiestas than classes. She offered the students food and drink, and frequently went with them to movies when the classes were over. She also encouraged her students to broaden their scope by reading writers such as Walt Whitman and the Russian poet Vladimir Mayakovsky and by studying pre-Columbian art as well as European artists, whom she introduced to them through her extensive collection of art books.

One of the most exciting projects that Frida arranged for her students was the painting of a *pulqueria*, a bar that served the venerable Mexican drink called *pulque*, the cheapest and crudest variant of fermented agave (tequila is *pulque's* better-known cousin). There were, and are, thousands of *pulquerias* in Mexico City, but the one Frida chose was near her house in Coyoacán.

It had the angelic name La Rosita, the little rose.

Most *pulquerias* have some kind of crude mural painted on their outside walls. This was a Mexican folk arts tradition that Frida wanted her students to appreciate and have fun with. Accordingly, she assigned them the task of creating and executing a composition about La Rosita to be painted on the building's outer walls. The students also wrote and drew art for a broadside in the style of José Posada announcing an "opening" upon completion of the project:

> The spectator! with his chitchat on the news of the day. Kind radio listeners: Saturday the 19th of June, at 11 in the morning. Grand premier of the Decorative paintings of the Gran Pulqueria La Rosita on the corner of Aguayo and Londres, Coyoacán, D.F. . . . The distinguished clientele of this house [will be offered] an exquisite barbecue imported directly from Texcoco. Add to the charm of this festival a band of Mariachis . . . sky rockets, firecrackers, invisible balloons, parachutists made of maguey leaves. . . . Exquisite *pulques*, lavish prizes, pretty girls, superior quality, painstaking attention.[2]

Los Fridos continued to study and work with Frida into the late 1940s and early 1950s. With Frida's assistance, they secured several other public mural projects, one of them sponsored by the national government, the painting of themes about laundry workers at several government-built public laundries (constructed so that women who made a living doing laundry would not have to work outside in streams). Later they would individually stay in touch with Frida and often drop by to visit.

Poor health had required Frida to cut back on her teaching and conduct her classes at her home. The pain in Frida's back and right foot, which in the past would lessen for periods of a year or more, had returned and this time did not leave her. As the pain persisted she became increasingly desperate for a cure. More and more in her letters to friends, the name of doctors begin to appear: Dr. Zimbrón, Dr. Ramíriz Moreno, Dr. Wilson, Dr. Farrill. But she was caught in a downward spiral: each new procedure, every innovative operation only caused her greater torment.

In 1944, Dr. Zimbrón devised a steel corset for her to wear which, he hoped, would support her back and lessen her pain. It offered only the slightest relief. She lost her appetite, dropped thirteen pounds in six months, and experienced fainting spells. Zimbrón then ordered her to undergo spinal injections. These worsened the pain and also caused her splitting headaches. Dr. Ramíriz Moreno examined her in 1945 and thought he had found the problem: syphilis. The cure was a series of blood transfusions and bismuth injections. The syphilis, if she had it, may have been cured. Her pain wasn't. She went back to Dr. Zimbrón who then tried an older method: he rigged her upright to a rack to stretch her spine. Bags of sand were tied to her feet. She was to remain in this device for three months and somehow still managed to paint for an hour every day. When that didn't work the doctors devised more corsets. Between 1944 and her death in 1954, she wore twenty-eight of them—one of steel, three of leather, twenty-four of plaster. One of them, put on her by an inexperienced doctor, began tightening on her like a boa constrictor during the night as it hardened. She had to get a house guest to cut it partially off to avoid asphyxiation.

By 1946 Frida was so desperate that she decided to return to the United States for an operation on her back. This procedure, the most drastic yet, was performed in New York by Dr. Philip Wilson. Wilson fused four of her vertebrae with bone removed from her pelvis and a fifteen-centimeter metal rod. According to several of Frida's later doctors, he also probably fused the wrong vertebrae. Again, this surgery worsened Frida's physical pain and emotional anguish. It also got her hooked on pain-killing narcotics.

It is impossible to give the true cause of Frida's suffering during this final decade of her life, if indeed there was something so simple as a single cause. Leo Eloesser believed her basic problem to have been scoliosis, the narrowing of the spine that could cause nerve damage. She may also have had a condition called osteomylitis, a progressive and incurable inflammation of the bone marrow. And, in one of her operations, she contracted a fungal infection of the bone that probably was never entirely cured. Her right foot also had been irremediably damaged in the 1927 trolley accident; throughout her life, it was subject to infections and unhealed sores that resulted from poor circulation and nerve damage and finally was amputated along with part of her right leg in 1953.

But her emotional state, which continued to fluctuate wildly and was tied to the condition of her relationship with Rivera, was a contributing factor as well. She had halfway extricated herself from him financially and was independent of him sexually in the sense that she took lovers as she pleased, yet they continued to be locked together in a strange, unbreakable emotional dependency. She remained, in Anita Brenner's words, "someone else's shadow." And Rivera was still, as Dr. Eloesser had suggested to her, exactly the same—childish and self-absorbed. He almost divorced her again in 1949 to marry the Mexican movie star María Felix. Frida's need for him, and her fear of abandonment by him, may have compelled her to make unwise medical decisions, ones that kept her ill and thus induced him to stay with her.

Their mother-son relationship, variously sad, and funny, was another way to try to possess him. He responded to it and it offered her a comfortable, if not odd, kind of emotional closeness.

The Broken Column, 1944.

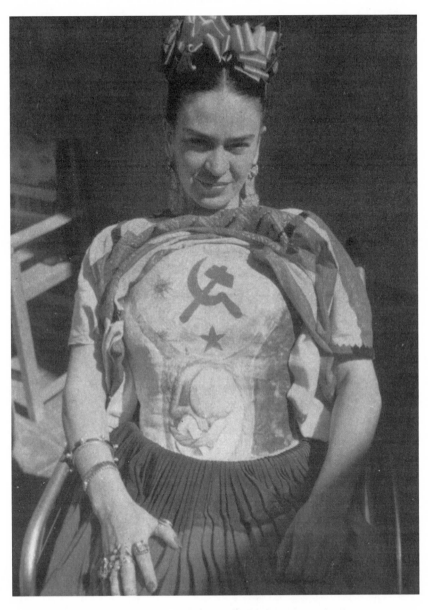

Frida in wheelchair wearing torso cast decorated
with hammer and sickle, ca. 1950.

When she was physically able, Frida liked to pamper Diego as a mother would pamper a child. She especially liked to give him baths. Because of his aversion to bathing, she had to coax him into the tub by placing his favorite floating bath toys in the water.

Another story illustrates Rivera's childishness and their mother-son dynamic. A friend and his child paid a visit to Frida one afternoon. Frida liked the child and let him play with one of Rivera's toy tanks, although she warned him "to keep it hidden if Diego comes . . . if he sees you playing with it, he will get angry." When Rivera did arrive, he reacted exactly as Frida predicted. According to the boy's father, Rivera's face "was like a little boy, almost crying."[3] Frida had to calm him and reassure him that she would get him other, nicer toys.

Yet this mother-son façade broke down when Frida was despairing and with her husband's increasing infidelities. According to Ella Wolfe, Bertram Wolfe's wife and Frida's longtime friend, "When I was alone with her she would tell me how sad her life was with Diego. She never got used to his loves. Each time the wound was new, and she kept on suffering till the day she died."[4]

Frida found a way to express her response to physical suffering in the painting *The Broken Column*, completed in 1944. In it she paints herself strapped to one of the corsets that Dr. Zimbrón had prescribed for her. She is naked from the waist up and a sheet reminiscent of a hospital bedsheet covers her hips and legs. Nails tacked into her body indicate pricks of pain. But the most dramatic aspect of the painting is her visualization of her wounded spine. She imagines it as a broken and barely functioning ionic column.

In spite of the tears covering her face, Frida looks straight at the viewer appearing almost brazen. Her features are expressionless and stoic, and she holds herself proudly upright. This is the face she wants to present to the world about her physical pain. She will suffer but not be bowed down or broken. It is a portrait of her fiercest side, representing her strong grasp on life; it is also a snapshot of her best days during the last decade of life. But, in the end, this attitude could not be sustained. "Life is replaced by a crumbling ruin," Frida wrote in her journal.

This awful pilgrimage of physical disintegration and surgical mutilation gained momentum in the late 1940s until it completely consumed Frida in the 1950s. She spent the entire year of 1950 in Mexico City's English Hospital where she underwent two more operations. With each setback her despair grew. Under the spell of painkilling narcotics, she began to lose her mental clarity and emotional stability, and her visual imagination gradually left her too. The ability to think about composition and intuit images deserted her. Increasingly she had nothing to nourish her except her newfound religion—Stalinist communism, and her illness. The former could not nurture her by itself; the latter proved bitterly corrosive.

In the last years of her life, it became clear that Frida needed a faith larger than the cult of Diego Rivera. Instinctively she chose communism as her religion and the Party as her church. Because she had never officially joined the Trotskyites, the Party readmitted her into its ranks in 1948, six years before it readmitted Rivera. And strangely, for a woman who in some ways was so aware of the injustices suffered by women at the hands of men, Frida adopted as her secular saints the all-male coterie of Marx, Lenin, Stalin, and Mao.

The last of Frida's paintings are crude embarrassments. In works such as *Marxism Will Give Health to the Sick*, painted in 1954, and her unfinished portrait of Stalin, it is clear the magical blend of personal mythology with Mexican folk art has disappeared. Her hand is also shaky. She no longer has the ability to paint fine, closely observed brush strokes.

Frida's brand of born-again communism was harsh and uncompromising. In the journal she kept in the last decade of her life, between despairing entries about her health and sanity, and visionary, almost Blakeian drawings of mythological creatures, she lurches back, as if pulled by a leash, to Party dogma. In March 1953, she writes, "Now in 1953, after 22 surgical interventions I feel better [this is the same year in which her right foot and part of her leg were amputated] and now and then I will be able to help my Communist Party. . . . For the first time in my life my painting is trying to help in the line set down by the Party. REVOLUTIONARY REALISM. . . . I am only a cell in the complex revolutionary mechanism." Three pages later, she says, "Dying. Coyoacán. THE WHOLE MEXICO THE WHOLE UNIVERSE has lost its balance with the loss [the passing] of STALIN. I always wanted to meet him personally but it no longer matters."

She was undoubtably fortunate never to make Stalin's acquaintance, especially if it would have coincided with an extended stay in the Soviet Union. Her imagination and naïvely ferocious nature were qualities that made for excellent gulag material. She might have ended up in the company of some of the people she had fought hardest to protect, refugees from the Spanish Civil War. Like Mexico, the Soviet Union had accepted a large number of left-wing Spaniards after the defeat of Republican forces. Unlike Mexico, the Soviet NKVD weeded through these to eliminate "undesirables." By 1942, a number of these Spaniards ended up in the gulag at Karaganda, north of Lake Balkhash in Kazakhstan. Originally known as the Karaganda State Farm, the camp was rechristened the Karaganda Special Corrective Labor Camp in a bureaucratic shuffling at the beginning of World War II. It was a harsh place on the steppes of central Asia. Record-keeping there was sporadic, but those very few who were eventually released reveal that most of their comrades died there of starvation and disease during the Second World War.[5]

This side of communism, the capricious, cruel, murderous side, was something that Frida decried as capitalist propaganda. She could not bear to admit that it was true. Nor could she admit the "error" of Stalin's continuing terror campaigns abroad, some of them conducted in Mexico. Julian Gorkin, a refugee from the Spanish Civil War and cofounder of the semi-Trotskyite Spanish Partido obrero de unificación marxista (better known by its acronym POUM), survived five attempts on his life, several of them in Mexico. In 1942, he wrote a deeply sardonic open letter to Mexican president Manuel Avila Camacho. "We solemnly declare," Gorkin proclaimed, "in response to whatever may befall us, that none of us suffers from a weak heart and none of us has any intention of committing suicide."

Perhaps what Frida could not bear to give up at this point in her life when everything else seemed to be falling apart was what Richard Wright called "passionate hope." Wright, an American writer, bemoaned this loss in himself when he quit the Party in the mid-1940s: "[I would] never be able to feel with the same sharpness about life, should never again express such passionate hope, should never again make so total a commitment of faith."[6]

Bertram Wolfe, Rivera's biographer, echoed Wright's feelings in his autobiography. Abandoning his Communist beliefs was

> a process rather than a single instantaneous act. . . . I did not lightly assume the task of communist organizer and educator. . . . The process was thoughtful, painful, and difficult . . . I longed to retain some shred of my old ideals and beliefs, longed to believe that I did not have to write off the spiritual investment of a decade as a total loss.[7]

With the loss of her health, her artistic vision, and always unsure whether Diego would desert her, Frida would not admit to a loss of faith in communism. Paradoxically, she, who struggled all her life to live free of controlling mores and rules, clutched to authoritarian Stalinist communism as her spiritual anchor.

In art, she would have one final triumph, this time fittingly in her native country. In April 1953, Lola Alvarez Bravo organized the only one-woman show of her work to be presented in Mexico during her life time. It was held at Bravo's Galería de Arte Contemporáneo, and Frida attended in her bed, which was moved from Coyoacán to downtown Mexico City and was included, with Frida in it, as part of the exhibition. Like a bejeweled and beribboned deity, Frida held court for all of Mexico that cared to show up to see her that night. "We asked people to keep walking," Alvarez Bravo recalls, "to greet her and then to concentrate on the exhibition itself. . . . There was really a mob—not only the art world, the critics, and her friends, but quite a lot of unexpected people." "It was," another friend said, "a little bit like a surrealist act, with Frida like the Spinx of the Night, presenting herself in the gallery in her bed. It was all theater."[8]

And it would be her last hurrah. The lines in Frida's diary chart her descent. On the upbeat days, she manages to execute some haunting drawings. On more desperate days, she writes hollow encomiums to Diego or the Party. On her worst days, those moments when she can clearly see that her life is ending, she lets loose startling, uncensored fragments of thought.

In one entry from 1953, between pages filled with propaganda in praise of Stalin, she has drawn a page full of faces. The entry says simply, "How ugly people are." Twenty-five pages later: "Diego. I'm so alone." Then, like a succession of bad dreams:

Color of poison. Everything upside down. . . . Mine was a strange world of criminal silences of strangers' watchful eyes misreading the evil. . . . I didn't live the NIGHTS. You are killing yourself. YOUR ARE KILLING YOURSELF!! . . . A very quiet passage that was leading me toward death . . .

I was so neglected! . . . Years. Waiting with anguish hidden away, my spine broken. . . . Carrying on my life enclosed in steel. . . . How can I explain to him my need for tenderness! My loneliness over the years. My structure displeases because of its lack of harmony, its unfitness. . . . If it were all over in an instant. I hope so. . . . Thanks to the doctors Farill — Glusker — Párres — Palomera Sanchez

Thanks to the nurses

to the stretcher bearers to the

cleaning women and attendants. . .

I hope the leaving is joyful—and I hope never to return.

FRIDA

Not long after this passage was written, Frida Kahlo took her leaving in the Blue House. The date was July 13, 1954. The probable cause of death was suicide by an overdose of narcotics.

Even though he was grief stricken and had locked himself into his room for hours at a time in the days after Frida's death, Diego Rivera managed to turn Frida's funeral into a Communist street parade. He saw to it that the red flag of communism, emblazoned with the hammer and sickle, was draped on her coffin. At the small crematorium at Panteon Civil de Dolores, Rivera led the mourners in singing the "Internationale," Lenin's funeral march, and other Communist songs.

When the cremation was finished, the ashes were gathered and returned to the Blue House, where they remain today, in an pre-Columbian urn shaped to resemble a headless, fecund woman, not the most fitting metaphor for Frida Kahlo's life.

During her too-brief forty-seven years, Frida Kahlo left a contradictory legacy. Intensely compassionate to friends and children, she was indifferent to the murder of millions in the name of her Communist faith. Wanting emotional closeness, she gave herself instead a distant husband. Yet in its wayward course, her life was no different from any other. But she left the world with one dazzling gift that only she could give, a measure of her flawed and brilliant life painted on tin and canvas, a keyhole into her soul, and perhaps if we look long enough, into ours too.

ACKNOWLEDGEMENTS

I first became aware of Frida Kahlo in the mid-1970s while I was a graduate student at the University of Texas Institute of Latin American Studies. There, in the institute's incomparable library, I saw reproductions of Kahlo's paintings and began to get an inkling of her complicated relationship with Diego Rivera.

Through the intervening years, I got to know even more about Kahlo through the rare showings of her paintings that I saw in New York City and through Hayden Herrera's excellent biography, *Frida: A Biography of Frida Kahlo*, and Herrera's book *Frida Kahlo: The Paintings*, which focuses more on Kahlo's art than her life. Even though these two books offer an exhaustive study of Kahlo, there seemed to be room for a condensed biography, one that captured Kahlo's conflicted spirit in a short but lively read. Thus I jumped at the chance to write this book when it was offered to me by the editors at Crossroad Publishing.

This work would not have been possible without the help of people who shared my passion for Kahlo and her art. Charles Lovell and Elisabeth Zarur, respectively director of the Art Gallery and professor of art history at New Mexico State University, were invaluable in sharing their knowledge of Mexican folk art. Crucial reference help was offered by Francis Mendoza and Margaret Soucy, librarians at Western New Mexico State

University. Finally, thanks to Barbara Leah Ellis, editor of Crossroad's *Lives & Legacies* series, and Gwendolin Herder, Crossroad's publisher, for believing that this book was necessary.

I would also like to thank the following people and institutions who opened their archives of art and photographs about Kahlo and her work: the Art Gallery of New Mexico State University, the Rockefeller Archive Center, Selma Ertegun, the Harry Ransom Humanities Research Center of the University of Texas at Austin, the Instituto Nacional de Bellas Artes of Mexico, and Throckmorton Fine Art of New York.

Those who would like to explore Kahlo's life and art in more detail should seek out two excellent primary source works, the *Diary of Frida Kahlo: An Intimate Self Portrait* and *Letters of Frida Kahlo*. For Kahlo the pop icon, an interesting work is Margaret Lindauer's *Devouring Frida*.

Informative books about Diego Rivera, and Kahlo and Rivera, include two works by Bertram Wolfe, *The Fabulous Life of Diego Rivera* and Wolfe's autobiography, *Life in Two Centuries*, as well as the recent biography of Rivera, Patrick Marnham's *Dreaming with His Eyes Open*. Of lesser value as a dependable account of historical events, yet entertaining nonetheless, is Rivera's autobiography *My Art, My Life*.

CHRONOLOGY

Note to reader: Events of Frida Kahlo's life appear on the left-hand side pages, and an historical chronology appears on the right-hand side pages.

1907   On July 6, Magdalena Carmen Frieda Kahlo y Calderón is born in Coyoacán, Mexico.

1913   Kahlo contracts polio. Her right leg is permanently affected and she is an invalid for almost a year.

1917   Kahlo witnesses fighting among competing armies in her neighborhood of Coyoacán in this sixth year of the Mexican Revolution.

1905 Diego Rivera graduates from the San Carlos Academy in Mexico City and begins a sixteen-year-long stay in Europe.

1910 In a month-long extravaganza, Porfirio Díaz celebrates the one-hundredth anniversary of Mexican Independence and his thirty-fourth year as president.
In November, Francisco Madero calls on Díaz to resign and announces the formation of a provisional revolutionary government.

1911 Border city of Ciudad Juárez falls to rebel forces; Díaz resigns and flees Mexico on May 25.

1912 U.S. troops intervene in Nicaragua to support a pro-U.S. president. American marines remain until 1925.

1913 Francisco Madero is assassinated. The bloodiest part of the Mexican Revolution begins.

1914 World War I begins in Europe in August.

1916 Francisco "Pancho" Villa raids Columbus, New Mexico, killing eight U.S. soldiers and ten civilians. The United States sends an "expeditionary" force, commanded by General John "Blackjack" Pershing after Villa.
The Dada movement, the precursor of Surrealism, founded in Zurich in 1916 by Tristan Tzara and friends.

1917 Dr. Atl hired as propagandist for Mexican warlord Venustiano Carranza.
In November Bolsheviks gain power in Russia.

1918 World War I ends in November.

1919 Emiliano Zapata, Mexican peasant revolutionary leader, assassinated.
As director of San Carlos Academy, Dr. Atl calls for a national mural project to extol revolutionary virtues.
Mexican Communist party founded.
In November, former general Alvaro Obregón elected president of Mexico, bringing an end to the Mexican Revolution.

1922 Kahlo enters Mexico's National Preparatory School, commuting to school in downtown Mexico City.
Meets Diego Rivera, who is working on his mural *Creation* in the school's auditorium.

1925 Kahlo begins art studies by apprenticing with commercial printer Fernando Fernández.
On September 17, while traveling with Gómez Arias on a city bus, Kahlo is seriously injured in a traffic accident.

1926 During a six-month period of bed rest, Kahlo completes her first painting: *Self-Portrait Wearing a Velvet Dress*.

1928 Kahlo meets Diego Rivera at a party given by Tina Modotti.

1929 Kahlo marries Rivera on August 21.
In October, Rivera is expelled from the Communist party; Kahlo also resigns, in sympathy with Rivera.

1930 Kahlo and Rivera live in Cuernavaca while Rivera works on a mural at the Cortés Palace.
In November Kahlo and Rivera journey to California where Rivera paints several murals in San Francisco.
Kahlo paints several portraits, including *Luther Burbank*, and a self-portrait for Dr. Leo Eloesser.

1931 Kahlo and Rivera return to the United States. In New York, they attend the opening for Rivera's retrospective at the Museum of Modern Art.

1932 In April, Kahlo and Rivera travel to Detroit where Rivera works on a mural at the Detroit Institute of Arts.
On July 4, Kahlo suffers a devastating miscarriage in Detroit. Later that month she paints *Henry Ford Hospital*.
In September Kahlo travels to Mexico to be with her ailing mother. Matilde Kahlo dies on September 14.
In October, at Diego Rivera's suggestion, Kahlo begins to paint episodes from her own life. The first one is entitled *My Birth*.

1920 José Vasconcelos named Mexican Minister of Education; begins an ambitious national mural program designed to glorify the heroes of the Revolution and Mexico's indigenous past.

1923 Pancho Villa assassinated.
Joseph Stalin becomes leader of Soviet government and Communist party.

1929 Mexican Communist party declared an illegal political organization.
Leon Trotsky, former Soviet revolutionary leader, exiled from Soviet Union.
In October, stock market crash in the United States begins the era known as the Great Depression.

1931 Stalin begins drive to eliminate independent Russian farmers; as a result, millions die of starvation over the next several years in the Soviet Union.

1933   Kahlo and Rivera travel to New York where Rivera has been commissioned to paint a mural at Rockefeller Center's RCA Building.

In May, after painting the face of Lenin on the New York mural, Rivera is evicted from the RCA Building and his mural contract is canceled.

In December, Kahlo and Rivera return to Mexico City.

1934   Kahlo terminates another pregnancy with an abortion.

In the summer, she separates from Rivera after discovering that he is having an affair with her sister Cristina.

1935   Kahlo travels to New York. When she returns to Mexico she engages in a brief affair with American sculptor Isamu Noguchi.

Partially in response to the pain she feels from Rivera's affair with her sister, Kahlo paints *A Few Small Nips.*

1936   Kahlo lives separately in her part of the San Angel studio. She takes an active part in aiding the Republican forces of the Spanish Civil War.

1937   Kahlo offers the Blue House in Coyoacán as a refuge for exiled Soviet revolutionary leader Leon Trotsky.

In June, Kahlo and Trotsky have a brief affair.

1938   Kahlo participates in the first public showing of her art at a group show in a small gallery in Mexico City.

Kahlo leaves for New York to attend her first one-woman show at the Julien Levy gallery.

Kahlo begins a serious relationship with New York fashion photographer Nickolas Muray.

1939   Kahlo travels to Paris to attend another showing of her work.

During the summer, Kahlo and Rivera separate again. She moves into the Blue House, where she will remain for the rest of her life.

Kahlo falls ill; while in a spinal traction, she paints *The Two Fridas.*

In December, Kahlo and Rivera divorce.

1933 Adolph Hitler comes to power in Germany.

1934 Populist former general Lázaro Cárdenas elected president of Mexico. During his six-year rule, he will nationalize U.S. oil companies and enact many progressive programs to aid Mexico's poor.

1936 Spanish Civil War begins.

1937 Show trials of thousands of Communist officials begin in Moscow. Most are executed or sent to Siberian prison camps.
Leon Trotsky is allowed to enter Mexico as a political refugee.

1939 In February, last Spanish Republican forces defeated; Spanish Civil War ends.
Stalin and Hitler sign nonaggression pact. Both of their armies invade Poland, which is divided between Germany and the Soviet Union.
World War II begins with declaration of war by the allies France and England on Germany.

1940 In May an attempt is made to assassinate Trotsky.
Fearing for his safety, Diego Rivera flees Mexico for San Francisco.
Trotsky is assassinated on August 20.
Kahlo travels to San Francisco to see Rivera and consult with Dr. Leo Eloesser.

1941 Kahlo's father Guillermo dies in April.

1942 Kahlo's work is included in a show "Twentieth-Century Portraits" at the Museum of Modern Art in New York City.

1943 Kahlo begins teaching art at the public secondary arts school La Esmeralda.

1944 Kahlo begins to experience major health problems; she begins a diary, which she will keep until her death.

1946 Kahlo undergoes a spinal fusion operation in New York City.

1948 Kahlo applies for, and is readmitted into, the Mexican Communist party.

1950 Kahlo spends most of the year in the English Hospital in Mexico City.

1951 Kahlo is confined full time to a wheelchair; she becomes addicted to pain-killing narcotics.

1953 Kahlo has her first one-woman show in Mexico at Lola Alvarez Bravo's Galería de Arte Contemporáneo.
Gangrene sets in to Kahlo's right foot; it is amputated in August.

1954 Kahlo dies on July 13 from a probable self-administered overdose of painkilling drugs.

1940   Germany conquers the Low Countries and France in
       May 1940.
       On the second try, Trotsky is killed by Stalinist agents in
       Mexico.

1941   Germany invades the Soviet Union in June.
       The Japanese attack Pearl Harbor in December; the
       U.S. declares war on Germany and Japan.

1945   Atomic age inaugurated by detonation of nuclear
       weapons over Japanese cities of Hiroshima and
       Nagasaki.
       World War II ends with surrender of Germany and
       Japan.

1953   Soviet dictator Joseph Stalin dies.

1957   Diego Rivera dies of cancer in Mexico City.

NOTES

CHAPTER 1: BLUE HOUSE

1. Tully, "The Kahlo Cult," *ARTnews* (April 1994), pp. 126–129.
2. Callcott, *Liberalism in Mexico*, p. 145.
3. Kandell, *La Capital: The Biography of Mexico City*, p. 376.
4. Quote from Frida Kahlo's half-sister, Maria Luisa Kahlo, in Hayden Herrera, *Frida: A Biography of Frida Kahlo*, p. 7.
5. As recalled by Kahlo's half-sister, Maria Luisa Kahlo, and another relative, Herrera, *Frida: A Biography*, p. 450, n. 11.
6. Tibor, *Frida Kahlo: An Open Life*, p. 30.
7. Ibid., p. 39.
8. These observations were made by Frida Kahlo's high school boyfriend, Alejandro Gómez Arias, and her half-sister, Maria Luisa Kahlo respectively, in Herrera, *Frida: A Biography*, p. 18.
9. Tibor, *Frida Kahlo: An Open Life*, p. 39.
10. Ibid., pp. 38–39.
11. Ibid., p. 38.
12. Herrera, *Frida: A Biography*, p. 37.
13. Tibor, *Frida Kahlo: An Open Life*, p. 38.

CHAPTER 2: CARNIVAL OF SKULLS

1. Kandell, *La Capital: The Biography of Mexico City*, p. 395.

2. Quotes from Kandell, *La Capital*, pp. 374–375.

3. Johns, *The City of Mexico in the Age of Díaz*, p. 44.

4. Quotes from Mexico City government reports, found in Johns, *The City of Mexico in the Age of Díaz*, p. 43.

5. Johns, *The City of Mexico in the Age of Díaz*, p. 110.

6. Tibor, *Frida Kahlo: An Open Life*, pp. 30–31.

7. Atkin, *Revolution: Mexico 1910–20*, p. 261.

8. Herrera, *Frida: A Biography of Frida Kahlo*, p. 36.

9. Manuel Gonzales Ramirez, quoted in Herrera, *Frida: A Biography*, p. 36.

10. This comment comes from Adelina Zendejas, one of Kahlo's friends at the National Preparatoria, in the film *The Life and Death of Frida Kahlo*, by Karen and David Crommie.

11. Rivera, *My Art, My Life: An Autobiography*, pp. 169–172.

CHAPTER 3: THE BALLERINA

1. Kahlo spelled her first name with an *e* until the early 1930s when Hitler's rise to power prompted her to drop the German spelling for a Spanish one. Kahlo's letter to Alejandro Gómez Arias is quoted in Hayden Herrera's *Frida: A Biography of Frida Kahlo*, p 35.

2. Ibid., pp. 38–39.

3. Ibid., p. 40.

4. Ibid., pp. 58–59.

5. From an interview with Gómez Arias in Herrera, *Frida: A Biography*, pp. 48–49.

6. Kahlo, *Letters of Frida Kahlo*, p. 25.

CHAPTER 4: MEXICAN DIONYSUS

1. Crane and Beals quotes from Helen Delpar, *The Enormous Vogue of Things Mexican*, pp. 79–80.

2. This quote from Wolfe cited in *Breaking with Communism*, p. 175.

3. Kahlo, *The Diary of Frida Kahlo: An Intimate Self-Portrait*, p. 19.

4. From an interview Kahlo gave with the Mexican journalist Bambi, "Frida Kahlo Es una Mitad," *Excelsior.*

5. Guillermo Kahlo quotes from Herrera's *Frida: A Biography of Frida Kahlo*, p. 172.

6. Bambi, "Frida Kahlo Es una Mitad," *Excelsior.*

CHAPTER 5: COLOSSUS OF THE NORTH

1. Rivera's observations about dress comes from *Time*, May 3, 1948, pp. 33–34.

2. Beloff quote cited in Marnham's, *Dreaming with His Eyes Closed: A Life of Diego Rivera*, p. 221.

3. Edward Weston, *Daybooks*, "California," vol. 2, pp. 198–199.

4. I am indebted to Carlos Fuentes's analysis of Xipe Totec from his introduction of Frida Kahlo's diaries.

5. Kahlo's letters to Leo Eloesser are quoted in Hayden Herrera, *Frida: A Biography of Frida Kahlo*, p. 138 and Kahlo, *Letters of Frida Kahlo.*

6. Source of Kahlo's letter to Rivera, papers of Bertram Wolfe, Hoover Institution, Stanford University.

CHAPTER 6: LA CHINGADA

1. Eloesser letter quoted in Hayden Herrera, *Frida: A Biography of Frida Kahlo*, p. 171.

2. Letter to Ella Wolfe, cited in Herrera, *Frida: A Biography*, p. 182.

3. Letter from Kahlo to the Wolfes, October, 18, 1934, in Kahlo, *Letters of Frida Kahlo*, p. 63.

4. Ibid., pp. 63–64.

5. Letter to Rivera from *Letters of Frida Kahlo*, pp. 67–68.

CHAPTER 7: THE PSEUDO-AMATEUR

1. Kahlo's letters to Lucienne Bloch quoted in Herrera's *Frida: A Biography of Frida Kahlo*, p. 225.

2. Breton, *Surrealism and Painting*, pp. 8, 144.

3. *Time*, November 14, 1939, p. 29.

4. Kahlo, *The Diary of Frida Kahlo*, p. 125–126.

5. Kahlo's letters to Muray quoted in Herrera's *Frida: A Biography*, pp. 245–246, 271.

6. I am indebted to Patrick Marnham for the concept of Kahlo and Rivera's "common vision" in his biography of Rivera, *Dreaming with His Eyes Open*.

CHAPTER 8: ON HER OWN TERMS

1. Leslie's remarks come from an interview with Hayden Herrera in Herrera, *Frida: A Biography of Frida Kahlo*, p. 275.

2. Description of *Sábado de Gloria* in turn-of-the-century Mexico City quoted in Michael Johns, *The City of Mexico in the Age of Díaz*, p. 84.

3. Quotes here and below from State Department papers at National Archives, College Park, Maryland.

4. Brenner's letter to Kahlo from Kahlo archive.

5. Rivera, *My Art, My Life*, p. 242.

CHAPTER 9: DEATH IS A FRIEND

1. Herrera, *Frida: A Biography of Frida Kahlo*, p. 329.
2. This broadside from the Frida Kahlo archive.
3. Herrera, *Frida: A Biography*, p. 376.
4. Ibid., p. 366.
5. Information about Spanish prison camp inmates in the Soviet gulag comes from David W. Pike, *In the Service of Stalin: Spanish Communists in Exile, 1939–1945*, pp. 161–165.
6. Wright, *Black Boy*, p. 210.
7. Wolfe from *Breaking with Communism*, pp. 9–10.
8. Herrera, *Frida: A Biography*, p. 409.

BIBLIOGRAPHY

BOOKS

Albers, Patricia. *Shadow, Fire, Snow: The Life of Tina Modotti*, New York: Clarkson Potter, 1999.

Costa-Amic, Bartomeu. *Leon Trotsky y Andreu Nin: dos asesinatos del Stalinismo*, Mexico: Altres-Costa-Amic, 1994.

Breton, André. "Frida Kahlo de Rivera," in *Surrealism and Painting*, translated by Simon Watson Taylor, New York: Harper & Row, 1972.

Callcott, Wilfred H. *Liberalism in Mexico, 1857–1929*, Hamden, Conn.: Archon Books, 1965.

Carmichael, Elizabeth, and Chloe Sayer. *The Skeleton at the Feast: Day of the Dead in Mexico*, Austin: University of Texas Press, 1992.

Carr, Barry. *Marxism and Communism in Twentieth-century Mexico*, Lincoln: University of Nebraska Press, 1992.

Delpar, Helen. *The Enormous Vogue of Things Mexican: Cultural Relations Between the United States and Mexico, 1920–1934*, Birmingham: University of Alabama Press, 1996.

Frank, Patrick. *Posada's Broadsheets: Mexican Popular Imagery, 1890–1910*, University of New Mexico Press, 1998.

Fuller, Samuel. *New York in the 1930s*, New York: Art Publishers, 1997.

Gómez Arias, Alejandro. "Un testimonio sobre Frida Kahlo," in *Frida Kahlo: Exposicion nacional de homenaje*, Instituto Nacional de Bellas Artes, Mexico City, 1977.

181

Heijenoort, Jean van. *Trotsky in Exile: From Prinkipo to Coyoacán*, Cambridge, Mass.: Harvard University Press, 1978.

Helm, MacKinley. *Mexican Painters: Rivera, Orozco, Siquieros and Other Artists of the Social Realist School*, New York: Dover, 1968.

Herrera, Hayden. *Frida: A Biography of Frida Kahlo*, New York: Harper and Row, 1983.

———. *Frida Kahlo: The Paintings*. New York: HarperCollins, 1991.

Hessen, Robert. *Breaking with Communism: The Intellectual Odyssey of Bertram Wolfe*, Palo Alto, Calif.: The Hoover Institution Press, 1990.

Johns, Michael. *The City of Mexico in the Age of Díaz*, Austin: University of Texas Press, 1997.

Kahlo, Frida, Sarah Lowe, and Carlos Fuentes. *Diary of Frida Kahlo: An Intimate Self Portrait*, New York: Harry Abrams, 1995.

Kahlo, Frida. *Letters of Frida Kahlo*, Edited by Martha Zamora, San Francisco: Chronicle, 1995.

Kandell, Jonathan. *La Capital: The Biography of Mexico City*, New York: Random House, 1988.

Levy, Julian. *Memoir of an Art Gallery*, New York: Putman, 1977.

Lindauer, Margaret. *Devouring Frida: Art History and Pop Celebrity of Frida Kahlo*, Wesleyan University Press, 1999.

Marnham, Patrick. *Dreaming with His Eyes Open: A Life of Diego Rivera*, New York: Knopf, 1998.

Pike, David W. *In the Service of Stalin: Spanish Communists in Exile, 1939–1945*, New York: Oxford University Press, 1993.

Poniatowska, Elena, and Carla Stellweg. *Frida Kahlo: The Camera Seduced*, San Francisco: Chronicle Books, 1991.

Richardson, Dan. *Comintern Army*, Lexington: University of Kentucky Press, 1982.

Rivera, Diego. *My Art, My Life: An Autobiography*, New York: Citadel, 1960.

Schumacker, Harris B. *Leo Eloesser M.D.: Eulogy for a Free Spirit*, New York: Philosophical Library, 1982.

Tibor, Raquel. *Frida Kahlo: An Open Life,* Translated by Elinor
    Randall, University of New Mexico Press, 1993.
Wald, Alan M. *The New York Intellectuals: Rise and Fall of the
    Anti-Stalinist Left from the 1930s to the 1980s,* Chapel
    Hill: University of North Carolina Press, 1987.
Weston, Edward. *Daybooks,* Millerton, N.Y.: Aperture, 1973.
Wolfe, Bertram D. *The Fabulous Life of Diego Rivera,* New York,
    Stein & Day, 1963.
———. *Life in Two Centuries: An Autobiography,* New York:
    Stein & Day, 1981.
Zamora, Martha. *Frida Kahlo: Brush of Anguish,* Translated by
    Marilyn Smith, San Francisco: Chronicle, 1995.

ARTICLES & CATALOGUES

Bambi. "Frida Kahlo es una mitad," *Excelsior* (Mexico City),
    June 13, 1954.
Grimberg, Salomon. *Frida Kahlo,* Exhibition catalog. The
    Meadows Museum, Southern Methodist University,
    Dallas, 1989.
Herrera, Hayden. "Frida Kahlo. Sacred Monsters," *Ms.* 6
    (February 1978): 29–31.
Frida Kahlo and Tina Modotti. Exhibition catalog. London:
    Whitechapel Gallery, 1982.
Kozloff, Joyce. "Frida Kahlo." *Women's Studies* 6 (1978): 43–59.
Orenstein, Gloria. "Frida Kahlo: Paintings for Miracles."
    Feminist Art Journal (Fall 1973): 7–9.
Tully, Judd. "The Kahlo Cult." *ARTnews* (April 1994): 126–29.
Wolfe, Bertram D. "Rise of Another Rivera." *Vogue,*
    (November 1, 1938): 64, 131.

BIBLIOGRAPHY

ARCHIVES

Hoover Institution on War Revolution and Peace, Stanford University, Palo Alto, California
> Information about Frida Kahlo's friend Bertram Wolfe and Diego Rivera's involvement with the Trotskyite Fourth International and Socialist Worker's Party can be found in the Hoover Institution's Hansen, Trotsky, Burnett Bolloten, and Joseph Freeman papers.

United States National Archives
> General Records of the State Department, 1940–44. Purport List 8–12-00B (reports to the consulate about Communist activity).

ILLUSTRATIONS

128   *The Two Fridas*, 1939. Oil on canvas, 29¼" x 38¾". Collection of the Museo de Arte Moderno, Mexico City. Courtesy of Schalkwijk/Art Resource, NY.

132   *Self-Portrait with Cropped Hair*, 1940. Oil on canvas, 15¾" x 11". Collection of the Museum of Modern Art, New York.

138   *The Dream*, 1940. Oil on canvas, 29¼" x 38¾". Collection of Selma Ertegun.

145   Frida, Leon and Natalia Trotsky, and contingent of undercover policemen at their arrival in Mexico City, 1937. Courtesy of Corbis.

150   Frida with her friend Teresa Proenza, 1952. Photo Bernice Kolko. Courtesy of Throckmorton Fine Art Inc., New York.

156   *The Broken Column*, 1944. Oil on masonite, 11" x 14¼". Collection of Dolores Olmedo Foundation, Mexico City. Courtesy of Schalkwijk/Art Resource, NY.

157   Frida in wheelchair wearing torso cast decorated with hammer and sickle, ca. 1950. Photo by Florence Aquina. Courtesy of Throckmorton Fine Art Inc., New York.

INDEX